Ars Amatoria;
Or,
The Art Of Love

by

Ovid

Ars Amatoria;
Or,
The Art Of Love
by Ovid

ISBN: 978-93-58592-09-2

Published by

DOUBLE 9 BOOKS

2/13-B, Ansari Road
Daryaganj, New Delhi – 110002
info@double9books.com
www.double9books.com
Tel. 011-40042856

ABOUT THE AUTHOR

Ovid was a Roman poet born on March 20, 43 BCE, in Sulmo, Italy. He was born into a wealthy family and received an education in Rome and Athens, studying rhetoric and literature. Ovid began his literary career as a poet of love elegies, including his most famous work, The Amores. He went on to write a number of other works, including the Metamorphoses, a narrative poem that tells the stories of mythological figures and their transformations, and the Fasti, a poetic calendar of Roman festivals and rituals. Ovid died in Tomis in 17 CE, and his works continued to be widely read and celebrated in the centuries that followed. He is regarded as one of the most important poets of the Roman era, known for his innovative and imaginative use of mythological themes and his skillful mastery of poetic form.

CONTENTS

BOOK -THE FIRST.

Should any one of the people not know the art of loving, let him read me; and taught by me, on reading my lines, let him love. By art the ships are onward sped by sails and oars; by art are the light chariots, by art is Love, to be guided. In the chariot and in the flowing reins was Automedon skilled: in the Hæmonian ship *of Jason* Tiphys was the pilot. Me, too, skilled in my craft, has Venus made the guardian of Love. Of Cupid the Tiphys and the Automedon shall I be styled. Unruly indeed he is, and one who oft rebels against me; but he is a child; his age is tender and easy to be governed. The son of Phillyra made the boy Achilles skilled at the lyre; and with his soothing art he subdued his ferocious disposition. He who so oft alarmed his own companions, so oft the foe, is believed to have stood in dread of an aged man full of years. Those hands which Hector was doomed to feel, at the request of his master he held out for stripes 701 as commanded. Chiron was the preceptor of the grandson of Æacus, I of Love. Both of the boys were wild; both of a Goddess born. But yet the neck of even the bull is laden with the plough; and the reins are champed by the teeth of the spirited steed. To me, too, will Love yield; though, with his bow, he should wound my breast, and should brandish his torches hurled against me. The more that Love has pierced me, the more has he relentlessly inflamed me; so much the fitter avenger shall I be of the wounds so made.

Phoebus, I pretend not that these arts were bestowed on me by thee; nor by the notes of the birds of the air am I inspired. Neither Clio nor the sisters of Clio have been beheld by me, while watching, Ascra, in thy vales, my flocks. To this work experience gives rise; listen to a Poet well-versed. The truth will I sing; Mother of Love, favour my design. Be ye afar, 702 ye with the thin fillets on your hair, the mark of chastity; and thou, long flounce, which dost conceal the middle of the foot. We will sing of guiltless delights, and of thefts allowed; and in my song there shall be nought that is criminal.

In the first place, endeavour to find out an object which you may desire to love, you who are now coming for the first time to engage as a soldier in a new service. The next task after that, is to prevail on the fair by pleasing her. The third is, for her love to prove of long duration. This is my plan; this space shall be marked out by my chariot; this the turning-place to be grazed by my wheels in their full career.

While you may, and while you are able to proceed with flowing reins; choose one to whom you may say, "You alone are pleasing to me." She will not come to you gliding through the yielding air; the fair one that suits must be sought with your eyes. The hunter knows full well where to extend the toils for the deer; full well he knows in what vale dwells the boar gnashing with his teeth. The shrubberies are known to the fowlers. He who holds out the hooks, knows what waters are swam in by many a fish. You, too, who seek a subject for enduring love, first learn in what spot the fair are to be met with. In your search, I will not bid you give your sails to the wind, nor is a long path to be trodden by you, that you may find her.

Let Perseus bear away his Andromeda from the tawny Indians, 703 and let the Grecian fair be ravished by Paris, the Phrygian hero. Rome will present you damsels as many, and full as fair; so that you will declare, that whatever has been on the earth, she possesses. As many ears of corn as Gargara has, as many clusters as Methymna; as many fishes as are concealed in the seas, birds in the boughs; as many stars as 704 heaven has, so many fair ones does your own Rome contain; and in her own City does the mother of Æneas hold her reign. Are you charmed by early and still dawning years, the maiden in all her genuineness will come before your eyes; or do you wish a riper fair, 705 a thousand riper will please you; you will be forced not to know which is your own choice. Or does an age mature and more staid delight you; this throng too, believe me, will be even greater.

Do you only saunter at your leisure in the shade of Pompey's Portico, 706 when the sun approaches the back of the Lion of Hercules; 707 or where the mother 708 has added her own gifts to those of her son, a work rich in its foreign marble. And let not the Portico of Livia 709 be shunned by you, which, here and there adorned with ancient paintings, bears the name of its founder. Where, too, are the grand-daughters of Be-lus, 710 who dared to plot death for their wretched cousins, and where their enraged father stands with his drawn sword. Nor let Adonis, bewailed by Venus, 711 escape you; and the seventh holy-day observed by the Jew of Syria. 712 Nor fly from the Memphian temples of Isis the linen-wearing heifer; she has made many a woman 713 that which she was herself to Jove. Even the Courts, (who would have believed it?) are favourable to Love; and oft in the noisy Forum has the flame been found. Where the erection 714 of Appius, 715 adjoining the temple of Venus, built of marble, beats the air with its shooting stream; 716 in that spot full oft is the pleader seized by Love; and he that has defended others, the same does not defend himself. Oft in that spot are their words found wanting to the eloquent man; and new cares arise, and his own cause has to be pleaded. From her temple, which is adjoining, 717 Venus laughs at him. He who so lately was a patron, now wishes to become a client.

But especially at the curving Theatres do you hunt for prey: these places are even yet more fruitful for your desires. There you will find what you may love, what you may trifle with, both what you may once touch, and what you may wish to keep. As the numberless ants come and go in lengthened train, when they are carrying their wonted food in the mouth that bears the grains; or as the bees, when they have found both their own pastures and the balmy meads, hover around the flowers and the tops of the thyme; so rush the best-dressed women to the thronged spectacles; a multitude that oft has kept my judgment in suspense. They come to see, they come that they themselves may be seen; to modest chastity these spots are detrimental.

Romulus, 'twas thou didst first institute the exciting games; at the time when the ravished Sabine fair 718 came to the aid of the solitary men. Then, neither did curtains 719 hang over the marble theatre, 720 nor was the stage 721 blushing with liquid saffron. There, the branches were simply arranged which the woody Palatium bore; the scene was void of art. On the steps made of turf sit the people; the branches promiscuously overshadowing their shaggy locks. They look about them, and they mark with their eyes, each for himself, the damsel which to choose; and in their silent minds they devise full many a plan. And while, as the Etrurian piper sends forth his harsh notes, the actor with his foot thrice beats the levelled ground; in the midst of the applause, (in those days applause was void of guile,) the King gives to his people the signal to be awaited for the spoil. At once, they start up, and, disclosing their intentions with a shout, lay their greedy hands upon the maidens. 722 As the doves, a startled throng, fly from the eagles, and as the young lamb flies from the wolves when seen; in such manner do they dread the men indiscriminately rushing on; the complexion remains in none, which existed there before. For their fear is the same; the symptoms of their fear not the same. Some tear their hair; some sit without consciousness; one is silent in her grief; another vainly calls upon her mother; this one laments; this one is astounded; this one tarries; that one takes to flight. The ravished fair ones are carried off, a matrimonial spoil; and shame itself may have been becoming to many a one. If one struggled excessively, and repelled her companion; borne off, the man himself lifted her into his eager bosom. And thus he spoke: "Why spoil your charming eyes with tears? What to your mother your father was, the same will I be to you." Romulus, 'twas thou alone didst understand how to give rewards to thy soldiers. Give such a reward to me, and I will be a soldier. In good truth, from that transaction, the festive Theatres, even to this day, continue to be treacherous to the handsome.

And let not the contest of the noble steeds escape you; the roomy Circus of the people has many advantages. There is no need there of fingers, with which to talk over your secrets; nor must a hint be taken by you through nods. Be seated next to your mistress, there being no one to prevent it; press your side to her side as close as ever you can; and conveniently enough, because the partition 723 compels you to sit close, even if she be unwilling; and because, by the custom of the place, the fair one must be touched by you. Here let the occasion be sought by you for some friendly chat, and let the usual subjects 724 lead to the first words. Take care, and enquire, with an air of Anxiety, whose horses those are, coming; and without delay, whoever it is to whom she wishes well, to him do you also wish well. But when the thronged procession shall walk with the holy statues of ivory, 725 do you applaud your mistress Venus with zealous hand. And, as often happens, if perchance a little dust should fall on the bosom of the fair, it must be brushed off with your fingers 726 and if there should be no dust, still brush off that none; let any excuse be a prelude to your attentions. If her mantle, hanging too low, shall be trailing on the earth, gather it up, and carefully raise it from the dirty ground. 727 At once, as the reward of your attention, the fair permitting it, her ancles will chance to be seen by your eyes. Look, too, behind, who shall be sitting behind you, that he may not press her tender back with his knee against it. 728 Trifles attract trifling minds. It has proved to the advantage of many a one, to make a cushion with his ready hand. 729 It has been of use, too, to waft a breeze with the graceful fan, and to place the hollow footstool beneath her delicate feet. Both the Circus, and the sand spread for its sad duties 730 in the bustling Forum, will afford these overtures to a dawning passion. On that sand, oft has the son of Venus fought; and he who has come to be a spectator of wounds, himself receives a wound. 731 While he is talking, and is touching her hand, and is asking for the racing list; 732 and, having deposited the stake, 733 is enquiring which has conquered, wounded, he sighs, and feels the flying dart, and, himself, becomes a portion of the spectacle so viewed.

Besides; when, of late, 734 Cæsar, on the representation of a rival fight, introduced 735 the Persian and Athenian ships; in truth, from both seas came youths, from both came the fair; and in the City was the whole of the great world. Who, in that throng, did not find an object for him to love? How many, alas! did a foreign flame torment? See! Cæsar prepares 736 to add what was wanting to the world subdued; now, remote East, our own shalt thou be! Parthian, thou shalt give satisfaction; entombed Crassi, rejoice; 737 ye standards, too, that disgracefully submitted to barbarian hands. Your avenger is at hand, and proves himself a general in his earliest years; and, while a boy, is conducting a war not fitted to be waged by a boy. Cease, in your fears, to count the birth-days of the Gods: 738 valour is the lot of the Cæsars, in advance of their years. The divine genius rises more rapidly than its years, and brooks not the evils of slow delay. The Tirynthian hero was a baby, and he crushed two serpents in his hands; even in his cradle he was already worthy of Jove. Bacchus, who even now art a boy, how mighty wast thou then, when conquered India dreaded thy thyrsi! With the auspices and the courage of thy sire, thou, Youth, shalt wield arms; and with the courage and the auspices of thy sire shalt thou conquer. Such first lessons are thy due, under a name so great; now the first of the youths, 739 at a future day to be the first of the men. Since thou hast brothers, 740 avenge thy brethren slain; and since thou hast a sire, 741 vindicate the rights of thy sire. He, the father of thy country and thine own, hath put thee in arms; the enemy is tearing realms away from thy reluctant sire. Thou wilt wield the weapons of duty, the foe arrows accursed; before thy standard, Justice and Duty will take their post. By the badness of their cause, the Parthians are conquered; in arms, too, may they be overcome; may my hero add to Latium the wealth of the East. Both thou, father Mars, and thou, father Cæsar, grant your divine favour as he sets out; for the one of you is now a Deity, thou, the other, wilt so be.

What, Parthian, dost thou leave to the conquered, who dost fly that thou mayst overcome? Parthian, even now has thy mode of warfare an unhappy omen. And will that day then come, on which thou, the most graceful of all objects, glittering with gold, shalt go, drawn by the four snow-white steeds? Before thee shall walk the chiefs, their necks laden with chains; that they may no longer, as formerly, be secure in flight. The joyous youths, and the mingled fair, shall be looking on; and that day shall gladden the minds of all. And when some one of the fair shall enquire the names of the Monarchs, what places, what mountains, or what rivers are borne in the procession; answer to it all; and not only if she shall make any inquiry; even what you know not, relate, as though known perfectly well. *

This is the Euphrates, 742 with his forehead encircled with reeds; the one whose 743 azure hair is streaming down, will be the Tigris. Make these to be the Armenians; this is Persia, sprung from Danaë; 744 that was a city in the vales of Achæ-menes. This one or that will be the leaders; and there will be names for you to call them by; correctly, if you can; if not, still by such as suggest themselves.

Banquets, too, with the tables arranged, afford an introduction; there is something there besides wine for you to look for. Full oft does blushing Cupid, with his delicate arms, press the soothed horns of Bacchus there present. And when the wine has besprinkled the soaking wings of Cupid, there he remains and stands overpowered on the spot of his capture. He, indeed, quickly flaps his moistened wings; but still it is fatal 745 for the breast to be sprinkled by Love. Wine composes to choose an object for you to love, where to lay your nets. Now, I attempt to teach you, by what arts she must be captured who has pleased you, a work of especial skill. Ye men, whoever you are, and in every spot, give attention eager to be informed; and give, all people, a favourable ear to the realization of my promises. First of all, let a confidence enter your mind, that all women may be won; you will win them; do you only lay your toils. Sooner would the birds be silent in spring, the grasshoppers in summer, sooner would the Mænalian dog turn its back upon the hare, than the fair, attentively courted, would resist the youth. She, however, will wish you to believe, so far as you can, that she is reluctant.

Lo! I utter a prophecy; thou wilt conquer, and I shall offer the lines which I have vowed; and with a loud voice wilt thou have to be celebrated by me. Thou wilt there he taking thy stand, and in my words thou wilt be animating thy troops. O that my words may not prove unworthy of thy spirit! I will celebrate both the backs of the Parthians as they fly, and the valour of the Romans, and the darts and the feelings, and makes them ready to be inflamed; care flies, and is drenched with plenteous wine. Then come smiles; then the poor man resumes his confidence then grief and cares and the wrinkles of the forehead depart. Then candour, most uncommon in our age, reveals the feelings, the God expelling *all* guile. On such occasions, full oft have the fair captivated the hearts of the youths; and Venus amid wine, has proved flames in flame. Here do not you trust too much to the deceiving lamp; 746 both night and wine are unsuited to a judgment upon beauty. In daylight, and under a clear sky, did Paris view the Goddesses, when he said to Venus: "Thou, Venus, dost excel them both." By night, blemishes are concealed, and pardon is granted to every imperfection; and that hour renders every woman beauteous. Consult the daylight about jewels, about wool steeped in purple; consult the daylight about the figure and the proportion.

Why enumerate the resorts of fair ones suited for your search? The sands would yield to my number. Why mention Baiæ, 747 and the shores covered with sails, and the waters which send forth the smoke from the warm sulphur? Many a one carrying thence a wound in his breast, has exclaimed; "This water was not so wholesome as it was said to be." See, too, the temple in the grove of suburban Diana, and the realms acquired with the sword by hostile hand. 748 Because she is a virgin, because she hates the darts of Cupid, she has given many a wound to the public, *and* will give many *still.*

Thus far, Thalia borne upon unequal wheels, 749 teaches where the foeman hurls from his flying steed.

As stealthy courtship is pleasing to the man, so, too, is it to the fair. The man but unsuccessfully conceals his passion; with more concealment does she desire. Were it agreed among the males not to be the first to entreat any female, the conquered fair would soon act the part of the suppliant. In the balmy meads, the female lows after the bull; the female is always neighing after the horny-hoofed horse. Passion in us is more enduring, and not so violent; among men the flame has reasonable bounds. Why mention Byblis, who burned with a forbidden passion for her brother, and who resolutely atoned with the halter for her crimes? Myrrha loved her father, but not as a daughter ought; and she now lies hid, overwhelmed by the bark 750 that grew over her. With her tears too, which she distils from the odoriferous tree, are we perfumed; and the drops still retain the name of their mistress.

By chance, in the shady vales of the woody Ida, there was a white hull, the glory of the herd, marked with a little black in the middle between his horns; there was but one spot; the rest was of the complexion of milk. The heifers of Gnossus and of Cydon 751 sighed to mate with him. Pasiphaë delighted to become the paramour of the bull; in her jealousy she hated the beauteous cows. I sing of facts well known: Crete, which contains its hundred cities, untruthful as it is, 752 cannot gainsay them. She herself is said to have cut down fresh leaves and the tenderest grass with hand unused to such employment.

She goes as the companion of the herds; so going, no regard for her husband restrains her; and by a bull 753 is Minos conquered. "Of what use, Pasiphaë, is it to put on those costly garments? This love of thine understands nothing about wealth. What hast thou to do with a mirror, when accompanying the herds of the mountain? Why, foolish one, art thou so often arranging thy smoothed locks? Still, do thou believe that mirror, that denies that thou art a heifer. How much couldst thou wish for horns to spring up upon thy forehead! If Minos still pleases thee, let no paramour be sought; but if thou wouldst rather deceive thy husband, deceive him through a being that is human."

Her chamber abandoned, the queen is borne over the groves and the forests, just as a Bacchanal impelled by the Aonian God. Alas! how oft with jealous look does she eye a cow, and say, "Why is she thus pleasing to my love? See how she skips before him on the tender grass! I make no doubt that the fool thinks that it is becoming to her." Thus she spoke, and at once ordered her to be withdrawn from the vast herd, and, in her innocence, to be dragged beneath the bending yoke; or else she forced her to fall before the altars, and rites feigned for the purpose; and, with joyous hand, she held the entrails of her rival. How often did she propitiate the Deities with her slain rivals, and say, as she held the entrails, "Now go and charm my love!" And sometimes she begged that she might become Europa, sometimes Io; because the one was a cow, the other borne upon a bull. Still, deceived by a cow made of maple-wood, the leader of the herd impregnated her; and by the offspring was the sire 754 betrayed.

If the Cretan dame 755 had withheld from love for Thyestes (alas! how hard it is for a woman possibly to be pleasing to one man only!) Phoebus would not have interrupted his career in the midst, and, his chariot turned back, retreated, with his returning steeds, to the morn. The daughter, who spoiled 756 Nisus of his purple locks, presses beneath her thigh and groin the raving dogs. The son of Atreus, who escaped from Mars by land, and Neptune on the waves, was the mournful victim of his wife. By whom have not been lamented the flames 757 of the Ephyrean Creusa? Medea, the parent, too, stained with the blood of her children? Phoenix, the son of Amyntor, 758 wept with his blinded eyes; you, startled steeds, tore Hippolytus in pieces. Why, Phineus, dost thou tear out the eyes of thy guiltless sons? 759 That punishment will revert to thy own head.

All these things have been caused by the passion of females. It is more violent than ours, and has more frenzy *in it*. Come then, and doubt not that you can conquer all the fair: out of so many, there will be hardly one to deny you. What they yield, and what they refuse, still are they glad to be asked for. Even if you are deceived, your repulse is without danger. But why should you be deceived, since new pleasures are delightful, and since what is strange attracts the feelings more than what is one's own? 760 The crop 761 of corn is always more fertile in the fields of other people; and the herds of our neighbours have their udders more distended.

But first, be it your care to make acquaintance with the handmaid of the fair one to be courted; she can render your access easy. 762 Take care that she is deep in the secrets of her mistress, and not too little entrusted with her secret frolics. Her do you bribe with promises, her with entreaties; you will obtain what you ask with little trouble, if she shall be willing. Let her choose the time (physicians, even, watch their time) when the feelings of her mistress are pliant, and easy to be influenced. Then will her feelings be easily influenced, when, in the best humour in the world, she shall be smiling, just as the corn on the rich soil. While hearts are joyous, and not closed by sadness, *then* are they assailable; then with soothing arts does Venus steal on apace. At the time when Troy was in sorrow, she was defended by arms;

when joyous, she admitted the horse pregnant with its soldiers. Then, too, must she be assailed, when she shall be fretting on being offended by a rival; then effect it by your means that she go not unrevenged. Let her handmaid, as she combs her hair in the morning, urge her on; and to the sail let her add the resources of the oar. And, sighing to herself, let her say, in gentle murmurs: "In my idea, you yourself cannot pay him in return." 763 Then let her talk about you; then let her add persuasive expressions; and let her swear that you are perishing with frantic passion. But speed on, let not the sails fall, and the breezes lull: like brittle ice, anger disappears in lapse of time.

You inquire if it is of use 764 to win the handmaid herself? In such attempts there is a great risk. This one becomes *more* zealous after an intrigue; that one more tardy; the one procures you as a gift for her mistress, the other for her own self. The result is doubtful; although she should favour your advances, still it is my advice, to refrain from so doing. I shall not go over headlong *tracks*, and over sharp crags; and, under my guidance, no youth shall be deceived. Even if she pleases you, while she gives and receives the letters, by her person, and not only by her zealousness alone; take care and gain her mistress first; let the other follow as her companion; your courtship must not be commenced with a servant-maid. This one thing I advise you (if you only put some trust in my skill, and if the boisterous wind does not bear my words over the seas): either do not attempt, or else do you persist; the informer is removed, when once she herself has shared in the criminality. The bird does not easily escape when its wings are bird-limed; the boar does not readily get away from the loose nets: the wounded fish can be held by the hook it has seized. Once tried, press her hard, and do not retreat, but as the conqueror. Then, guilty of a fault that is common to you both, she will not betray you; and the sayings and doings of her mistress will be well known to you. But let this be well concealed; if your informant shall be well concealed, your mistress will ever be under your eye.

He is mistaken who supposes that time is the object of those only who till the fields, and is to be observed by mariners alone. Neither must the corn be always trusted to the treacherous soil; nor the hollow ships at all times to the green waves; nor is it safe to be ever angling for the charming fair. The same thing may often be better done when an opportunity offers. Whether it is her birthday 765 that comes, or whether the Calends, 766 which Venus delights to have as the successor of the month of Mars; or whether the Circus shall be adorned, not with statues, as it was before, but shall be containing the wealth of kings 767 exposed to view; delay your project; then the storm is boisterous, then the Pleiades prevail; 768 then, the tender Kid is sinking in the ocean wave. Then, 'tis well to desist; then, if one trusts the deep, with difficulty he grasps the shipwrecked fragments of his dismantled bark. You may make a beginning on the day on which tearful Allia 769 was stained with the blood of the Latian wounds; on the day, too, when the festival recurs, observed each seventh day by the Syrian of Palestine, a day not suited for 770 the transaction of business.

Great must be 771 your dread of the birthday of your mistress, and unlucky be that day on which any present must be made. Though you should cleverly avoid her, still she will spoil you; a woman finds contrivances, by means of which to plunder the riches of the eager lover. The loosely-clad pedlar 772 will be coming to your mistress, so fond of buying, and while you are by, will be exposing his wares. She wills ask you to examine them, only that you may appear to be knowing; then she will give you a kiss, and then entreat you to purchase. She will swear that she will be content with this for many a year; she will say that now she has need of it, now it may be bought a bargain. If you shall make the excuse that you have not the money at home to give; a promissory note 773 will be asked for; it would then profit you not to have learned 774 to write. Besides, too; when she asks for a present, as though for the birth-day cake, 775 and is born for her own pleasure as often as she pleases. And further; when, full of tears, she laments her pretended loss, and the jewel 776 is feigned to have fallen from her pierced ear. They ask for many a sum to be lent them; so lent, they have no inclination to return them. You lose the whole; and no thanks are there for your loss. Had I ten mouths, with tongues as many, they would not suffice for me to recount the abominable contrivances of courtesans.

Let the wax that is poured upon the polished tablets first try the ford; let the wax first go as the messenger of your feelings. Let it carry your compliments; and whoever you are, add expressions that feign you to be in love, and entreaties not a few. Achilles, moved with his entreaties, granted Hector to Priam; an angered Divinity is moved by the voice of entreaty. Take care to make promises: for what harm is there in promising? Any person whatever can be rich in promises. Hope, if she is only once cherished, holds out for a long time; she is, indeed, a deceitful Goddess, but still a convenient one. Should you give her 777 anything, you may for that reason be abandoned by her: she will bear off the gift by-gone, and will have lost nothing in return. But that which you have not given, you may always seem as though about to give; thus has the sterile field full oft deceived its owner. So the gambler, in order that he may not lose, does not cease to lose; and the alluring dice ever recall the anxious hand. This is the task, this the labour; to gain her without even the first present. What she has once given, she will always give, that she may not have granted to no purpose. Let the letter go then, and let it be couched in tender expressions; and let it ascertain her feelings, and be the first to feel its way. A letter borne upon an apple 778 deceived Cydippe; and by her own words the fair was unconsciously caught.

Youths of Rome, learn, I recommend you, the liberal arts; and not only that you may defend the trembling accused. Both the public, and the grave judge, and the silent Senate, as well as the fair, conquered by your eloquence, shall extend their hands. 779 But let your power lie concealed: and do not be eloquent at the first. Let your letters avoid difficult words. Who, but one bereft of sense, would declaim before a charming mistress? Full oft has a letter proved a powerful cause for hatred. Let your language be intelligible, and your words the usual ones; but pleasing, so that you may seem to be speaking in person. Should she not accept your letter, and send it back unread, hope that she will read it, and persist in your design. In time the stubborn oxen come beneath the ploughs: in time the steeds are taught to submit to the flowing reins: by continued use the ring of iron 780 is consumed: by being in the ground continually, the crooked plough is worn out. What is there harder than stone? What more yielding than water? Yet hard stones are hollowed out by yielding water. Only persist, and in time you will overcome Penelope herself. You see that Pergamus was taken after a long time; still, it was taken.

If she reads it, and will not write in answer, do not attempt to compel her. Do you only make her to be continually reading your flattering lines. What she has been pleased to read, she will be pleased to answer when read. *All* these things will come in their turn, and by degrees. Perhaps even, at first, a discouraging letter will come to you; and one that entreats you not to wish to molest her. What she entreats you *to do*, she dreads; what she does not entreat you *to do, namely*, to persist, she wishes you *to do*. Press on; and soon you will be the gainer of your desires. In the meantime, if she shall be carried lying along upon her couch, do you, as though quite by accident, approach the litter of your mistress; and that no one may give a mischievous ear to your words, cunningly conceal, them so far as you can in doubtful signs. If, with sauntering foot, the spacious Portico is paced by her; here, too, do you bestow your leisure in her attendance. And sometimes do you take care to go before; sometimes follow behind; and sometimes be in a hurry, and sometimes walk leisurely. And be not ashamed to pass from the throng under some of the columns, 781 or to walk with her, side by side. And let her not be seated long without you in the curving Theatre; in her shoulders she will bring something for you to be spectator of. Her you may gaze upon, her you may admire; much may you say by your brows, much by your gestures. Clap too, when the actor is dancing 782 in the part of some damsel; and whatever lover is represented, him applaud. Rise when she rises; sit as long as she is seated; employ your time at the caprice of your mistress.

But let it not please you to curl your hair with the irons: 783 and rub not your legs with the rough pumice. 784 Bid those do this, 785 in whose Phrygian notes the Cybeleian Mother is celebrated by their yells. A neglect of beauty becomes men, Theseus bore off the daughter of Minos, though his temples were bedecked by no crisping-pin. Phædra loved Hippolytus, 786 and he was not finely trimmed. Adonis, habituated to the woods, was the care of a Goddess. But let neatness please you; let your body be bronzed on the Plain of Mars: 787 let your robe be well-fitting, and without a spot. Let your tongue, too, not be clammy; 788 your teeth free from yellowness; and let not your foot wallop about, losing itself in the shoe down at heel. Let not the cutting shockingly disfigure your hair bolt upright; let your locks, let your beard be trimmed by a skilful hand. Let your nails, too, not be jagged, and let them be without dirt; and let no hairs project from the cavities of your nostrils. And let not the breath of your ill-smelling mouth be offensive; and let not the husband and the father of the flock 789 offend the nostrils. The rest, allow the luxurious fair to do; and any man that perchance disgracefully seeks to attract another.

Lo! Bacchus calls his own Poet: he, too, aids those who love; and he encourages the flame with which he burns himself. The Gnossian fair was wandering distractedly on the unknown sands, where little Dia is beaten by the ocean waves. And, just as she was *on awaking* from her sleep, 790 clothed in a loose tunic, with bare feet, and having her yellow hair loose, she was exclaiming to the deaf waves that Theseus was cruel, while the piteous shower of tears was moistening her tender cheeks. She exclaimed, and at the same moment she wept; but both became her, nor was she rendered unsightly by her tears. And now again beating her most beauteous bosom with her hands, she cried—"That perfidious man has gone; what will become of me?"

"What will become of me?" she said; when cymbals resounded over all the shore, and tambourines were beaten with frantic hand. She dropped down with alarm, and stopped short in her closing words; and no blood was there in her lifeless body. See! the Mimallonian females, 791 with their locks flowing on their backs; see! the nimble Satyrs, the throng preceding the God; sec! Silenus, the drunken old man, 792 on his bending ass, sits there with difficulty, and holds fast by the mane that he presses. While he follows the Bacchanals, the Bacchanals both fly and return: while the unskilful rider is goading on his animal with his stick, slipping from the long-eared ass, he tumbles upon his head. The Satyrs cry aloud, "Come, rise up; rise, father!" Now, the God, from his chariot, the top of which he had wreathed with grapes, loosened the golden reins for the tigers yoked to it. Both her complexion, and Theseus, and her voice forsook the fair one; and thrice she attempted flight, and thrice was she detained by fear. She shuddered, just as the barren ears of corn, which the wind shakes; just as the slender reed quivers in the swampy marsh.

To her the Divinity said, "Lo! I come to thee a more constant lover; damsel of Gnossus, lay aside thy fear, the wife of Bacchus shalt thou be. Receive heaven as my gift: a conspicuous Constellation in the heavens, full oft, Cretan Diadem, 793 shalt thou direct the veering bark." Thus he said; and he leapt from the chariot, that she might not be in dread of the tigers; the sand yielded to his foot placed upon it. And folding her in his bosom he bore her off; for to struggle she was unable: how easy 'tis for a God to be able to do anything. Some sing "Hymenæus," some cry "Evie, Evoë!" 794 Thus are the God and his bride united in holy wedlock.

Therefore, when the gifts of Bacchus placed before you fall to your lot, and the fair one shall be a sharer in the convivial couch; pray both to father Nyctelius, and his nocturnal rites, that they will bid the wine not to take effect on your head. Here, in secret discourse, you may say to her many a free word, which she may understand is addressed to her; and you may trace out short compliments with a little wine, so that she may read on the table 795 that she is your favorite; and look on her eyes with eyes that confess your flame; the silent features often have both words and expression. Take care to be the next to seize the cup that has been touched by her lips; and drink from the side 796 that the fair drinks from. And whatever food she shall have touched with her fingers, 797 do you reach for it; and while you are reaching, her hand may be touched by you. Let it also be your object to please the husband of the fair; *once* made a friend, he will be more serviceable for your designs. If you are drinking by lot, 798 grant him the first turn: let the chaplet, taken from your own head, be presented to him. Whether he is below you, or whether your neighbour, let him help Himself to every thing first; and do not hesitate to speak only after he has spoken. Secure and much frequented is the path, for deceiving through the name of friendship. Secure and much frequented though that path be; *still* it is to be condemned. For this cause 'tis that the agent attends even too much 799 to his agency, and thinks that more things ought to be looked after by him than those entrusted to him.

A sure rule for drinking shall be given you by me: let both your mind and your feet ever observe their duty. Especially avoid quarrels stimulated by wine, and hands too ready for savage warfare. Eurytion 801 met his death from foolishly quaffing the wine set before him. Banquets and wine are rather suited for pleasant mirth. If you have a voice, sing; if pliant arms, dance; and by whatever talent you can amuse, amuse. As real drunkenness offends, so feigned *inebriety* will prove of service. Let your deceiving tongue stutter with lisping accents; so that whatever you shall do or say with more freedom than usual, it may be supposed that excess of wine is the cause. And express all good wishes for your mistress; all good wishes for him who shares her couch; but in your silent thoughts pray for curses on her husband. But when, the tables removed, the guests shall be going, (the very crowd will afford you access and room) mix in the throng: and quietly stealing up 802 to her as she walks, twitch her side with your fingers; and touch her foot with your foot.

Now is the time come for some conversation: fly afar hence, coy bashfulness, let Chance and Venus befriend the daring. Let your eloquence not be subject to any laws of mine; only make a beginning, of your own accord you will prove fluent. You must act the lover, and wounds must be feigned in your words. Hence let confidence be sought by you, by means of any contrivances whatever. And 'tis no hard matter to be believed; each woman seems to herself worthy to be loved. Though she be ugly in the extreme, to no one are her own looks displeasing. Yet often, he that pretends to love, begins in reality: full oft he becomes that which in the beginning he feigned to be. For this cause, the rather, O ye fair, be propitious to those who pretend. That passion will become real, which so lately was feigned.

Now be it your part stealthily to captivate her affection by attentions; just as the shelving bank is encroached on by the flowing stream. Be not tired of praising either her face or her hair; her taper fingers too, and her small foot. The praise of their beauty pleases even the chaste; their charms are the care and the pleasure of even maidens. For, why, even now, are Juno and Pallas ashamed at not having gained the decision in the Phrygian groves? The bird of Juno 803 exposes her feathers, when praised; if you look at them in silence, she conceals her treasures. Amid the contests of the rapid course, their trimmed manes, and their patted necks, delight the steeds.

Promise, too, without hesitation: promises attract the fair: make any Gods you please to be witnesses of what you promise. Jupiter, from on high, smiles at the perjuries of lovers, and commands the Æolian South winds to sweep them away as worthless, Jupiter was accustomed to swear falsely to Juno by the Styx: now is he himself indulgent to his own precedent. 'Tis expedient that there should be Gods; 804 and as it is expedient, let us believe them to exist. Let frankincense and wine be presented on their ancient altars. No repose, free from care and similar to sleep, possesses them; live in innocence, for a Divinity is ever present. Restore the pledge; let piety observe her duties; be there no fraud; keep your hands free from bloodshed.

Deceive, if you are wise, the fair alone with Impunity; for this one piece of deceit only is good faith to be disregarded. Deceive the deceivers; in a great measure they are all a guilty race; let them fall into the toils which they have spread. Egypt is said to have been without showers that refresh the fields: and to have been parched during nine years. When Thrasius went to Busiris, 805 and showed that Jupiter could be propitiated by shedding the blood of strangers; to him Busiris said, "Thou shalt become the first sacrifice to Jove, and, a stranger, thou shalt produce rain for Egypt." Phalaris, too, burnt in the bull the limbs of the cruel Perillus; the unhappy inventor was the first to make proof of his work. Each of them was just; and, indeed, no law is there more righteous, than that the contrivers of death should perish by their own contrivances. Therefore, since perjuries with justice impose upon the perjured, let woman grieve, deceived through a precedent her own.

Tears, too, are of utility: by tears you will move adamant. Make her, if you can, to see your moistened cheeks. If tears shall fail you, for indeed they do not always come in time, touch your eyes with your wet hand. What discreet person would not mingle kisses with tender words? Though she should not grant them; still take them ungranted. Perhaps she will struggle at first, and will say, "You naughty man!" still, in her struggling, she will wish to be overcome. Only, let them not, rudely snatched, hurt her tender lips, and take care that she may not be able to complain that they have proved a cause of pain. He who has gained kisses, if he cannot gain the rest as well, will deserve to lose even that which has been granted him. How much is there wanting for unlimited enjoyment after a kiss! Oh shocking! 'twere *downright* clownishness, and not modesty. Call it violence, if you like; such violence is pleasing to the fair; they often wish, through compulsion, to grant what they are delighted *to grant*. Whatever fair one has been despoiled by the sudden violence of passion, she is delighted at it; and the chief is as good as a godsend. But she, who, when she might have been carried by storm, has escaped untouched, though, in her features, she should pretend gladness, will *really* be sorry. Phoebe suffered 806 violence; to her sister was violence offered; and pleasing was either ravisher to the ravished. The damsel of Scyros being united to the Hæmonian hero, is a well-known story indeed, but not unworthy to be related.

Now, the Goddess, worthy to conquer the other two at the foot of mount Ida, had given her reward of the approval of her beauty. Now, from a distant region, had a daughter-in-law come to Priam: and within Ilian walls there was a Grecian wife. All swore in the words of the affronted husband; for the grief of one was the common cause. A disgraceful thing, had he not yielded in this to the entreaties of his mother, Achilles had concealed his manhood by the long garments. What art thou doing, descendant of Æacus? The wool is no task of thine. Do thou seek glory by other arts of Pallas. What hast thou to do with work-baskets? 807 Thy hand is fitted for holding the shield. Why hold the allotted flax in thy right hand, by which Hector shall fall? Spurn those spindles enwrapped in the laborious warp; the lance from Pelion is to be brandished by that hand. By chance in the same chamber there was a royal maiden; in her own undoing she found that he was a male. By force, indeed, was she overcome, so we must believe: but still, by force was she willing to be overcome. Many a time did she say, "Stay," when now Achilles was hastening *to depart*; for, the distaff laid aside, he had assumed valiant arms. Where now is this violence? Why, with gentle voice, Deidamia, dost thou detain the perpetrator of thy disgrace? As, forsooth, there is shame in first beginning at any time, so 'tis pleasing *to the fair* to submit, when the other takes the initiative.

Alas! too great is the confidence of any youth in his own good looks, if he awaits for her to be the first to ask him. Let the man make the first approaches; let the man use words of entreaty; she will kindly receive his soft entreaties. To gain *your wish*, ask; *she only wishes to be asked*. Tell her the cause and the origin of your desires. Jupiter came as a suppliant to the Heroines of olden times; 808 no fair one found fault with great Jove. But if you perceive puffed-up vanity to be the result of your prayers, desist from your design, and withhold your advances. Many desire that which flies from them, and hate that which is close at hand. By pressing on less eagerly, remove all weariness of yourself. Nor must your hope of enjoyment be always confessed by you as you entreat; let Love make his entrance concealed beneath the name of friendship. By this introduction, I have seen the prudish fair deceived; he who was the friend, became the lover. A fair complexion is unbecoming in a sailor; he ought to be swarthy, from the spray of the sea and the rays of the sun. It is unbecoming, too, to the husbandman, who, with his crooked plough and his heavy harrows, is always turning up the ground in the open air. And if your body is fair, you, by whom the glory of the chaplet of Pallas 809 is sought, you will be unsightly.

Let every one that is in love be pale; that is the proper complexion for one in love. That is becoming; from your features, let the fair think that you are not in good health. Pale with love for Lyrice, 810 did Orion wander in the woods; pale for the Naiad, in her indifference, was Daphnis. 811 Thinness, too, shows the feelings; and think it no disgrace to put a hood over your shining looks. Let sleepless nights attenuate the bodies of the youths; care, too, and the grief that proceeds from violent love. That you may gain your desires, be wretched, that he who sees you may be able to say, "You are in love."

Shall I complain, or *only* remind you how all right and wrong is confused? Friendship is but a name, constancy an empty title. Alas! alas! it is not safe to praise the object that you love to your friend. When he has credited your praises, he supplants you. But the descendant of Actor did not defile the couch of Achilles; so far as Pirithous was concerned, Phædra was chaste. Pylades 812 loved Hermione, with the affection with which Phoebus loved Pallas; and he was such, daughter of Tyndarus, as thy twin brother Castor was towards thee. If any one expects the same, let him expect that the tamarisks will bear apples, and let him look for honey in the middle of the stream. Nothing pleases but what is base; his own gratification is the object of each. This, too, becomes pleasant from the sorrow of another. Oh disgraceful conduct! no enemy is to be dreaded by the lover. Shun those whom you think trustworthy; then you will be safe. Shun your kinsman, and your brother, and your dear friend; this class will cause you real alarm.

I was *here* about to conclude; but there are various dispositions in the fair; treat these thousand dispositions in a thousand *different* ways. The same soil does not produce everything; one suits the vine, another the olive; in this, corn springs up vigorously. There are as many characters in these various dispositions, as there are forms in the world; the man that is wise, will adapt himself to these innumerable characters. And as at one moment Proteus will make himself flow in running water; and now will be a lion, now a tree, now a shaggy goat. These fish are taken with a dart, 813 those with hooks; these the encircling nets draw up, the rope being extended. And let no one method be adopted by you for all years. The aged hind will espy from a greater distance your contrivances. Should you seem learned to the ignorant, or forward to the bashful, she will at once distrust herself, now apprehensive. Thence it happens, that she who has dreaded to trust herself to the well-bred man, *often* falls into the embrace of some worthless inferior.

A part remains of the task which I have undertaken, a part is completed; here let the anchor, thrown out, hold fast my bark.

BOOK -THE SECOND.

Sing, "Io Pæan" 901 and "Io Pæan" twice sing; the prey that was sought has fallen into our toils. Let the joyous lover present my lines with the verdant palm; to *Hesiod* the Ascræan and to *Homer* the Mæonian old man shall I be preferred. Such did the stranger son of Priam set his whitening sails from the armed Amyclæ, 902 together with the ravished wife. Such was he who bore thee, Hippodamia, in his victorious chariot, carried by the wheels of the stranger. Why hasten then, young man? Thy ship is sailing in the midst of the waves; and far distant is the harbour for which I make. It is not enough, me your Poet, for the fair to be gained by you. Through my skill has she been acquired; through my skill must she be retained. 'Tis no less merit to keep what is acquired, than to gain it. In the former there is some chance; in the latter will be a work of art.

Now, if ever, Boy *Cupid* and Cytherea, be propitious *to me*: now, Erato; 903 for thou hast a name from Love. Great attempts do I contemplate; to tell by what means Love can be arrested, the Boy that wanders over the world so wide. He is both inconstant, and he has two wings with which to fly.'Tis an arduous task to impose laws on these.

Minos had obstructed all means of escape to the stranger. He discovered a bold path 904 with his wings. When Dædalus had enclosed the man half-bull, and the bull half-man, that was conceived in the criminality of his mother; he said, "Most just Minos, let there be a termination of my exile; and let my paternal land receive my ashes. And since, harassed by the cruel Destinies, I cannot live in my country, let me be enabled to die. If the merits of an old man are but small, grant a return to this boy; if thou art unwilling to favour the boy, then favour the old man." This he said: but both this and many more things he might have said; the other did not permit a return to the hero. Soon as he saw this, he said, "Now, O now, Dædalus, thou hast a subject, upon which thou mayst prove ingenious. Lo! Minos possesses the land, and he possesses the ocean; neither earth nor water is open for our escape; there remains a path through the heavens; through the heavens will we attempt to go. Jupiter on high, grant pardon to my design. I do not aim to reach the starry abodes; there is no way but this one, by which I may escape the tyrant. Should a road through Styx be granted; then we will swim through the Stygian waves; let the laws of nature be changed by me."

Misfortunes often sharpen the genius; who could have ever believed, that a mortal could attempt the paths of the air?

He arranges swift feathers in order, like oars, 905 and connects the light work with fastenings of thread; the lower part, too, is bound together with wax, melted by the fire; and now the work of the new contrivance is finished. The smiling boy handles both the wax and the feathers, not knowing that these instruments are prepared for his own shoulders. To him his father says: "With these ships must we reach our native land; by these means must we escape from Minos. The air Minos could not, all else he has, shut against us. Cleave the air, which still thou mayst, with these my inventions. But neither the virgin of Tegeæa, nor the sword-bearing Orion, 906 the companion of Bootes, will have to be beheld by thee. Follow me with the wings given to thee: I will go before on the way. Be it thy care to follow; me thy leader, thou wilt he safe. But if we shall go through the air of the heavens, the sun close to us, the wax will not be able to endure the heat. If we shall wave our wings below, the sea near to us, the fluttering feathers will be wet with the ocean spray. Fly between them both; dread, too, the winds, my son; and whichever way the breezes shall blow, set thy prospering sails."

While he thus advises; he fits his work on to the boy, and shows how it is to be moved; just as their mother teaches the helpless birds. Then he places upon his shoulders the wings made for himself; and with timidity he poises his body along this new track. And now about to fly, he gives kisses to his little son; and the cheeks of the father do not withhold their tears. There is a hill, less than a mountain, more lofty than the level plain; hence are their two bodies entrusted to their mournful flight. Dædalus both moves his own wings himself, and looks back on those of his son; and he ever keeps on his own course. And now this unusual path delights him, and, fear laid aside, Icarus flies more courageously with emboldened skill. A person sees them, while he is angling 907 for fish with his quivering rod, and his right hand desists from the work he has commenced. Now Samos and Naxos had been left behind, on the left hand, and Paros, and Delos beloved by the Clarian God. 908 Lebynthos was to the right, and Calymne 909 shaded with its woods, and Astypalæa, 910 surrounded with its fishy shallows; when the boy, too venturesome in his inconsiderate daring, took a higher flight, and forsook his guide.

The fastenings give way; and the wax melts, the Divinity being so near; and his arms, when moved, no longer catch the light breeze. Alarmed, he looks down upon the sea from the lofty heavens; darkness, arising from trembling apprehension, comes over his eyes. The wax has now melted; he waves his bare arms, and he trembles, and has no means whereby to be supported. Downward he falls; and as he falls, he cries, "Father! O father! I am undone!" As he spoke, the azure waves closed his mouth. But the unhappy father, a father now no longer, cried aloud, "Icarus, where art thou? Or under what part of the sky dost thou fly?"

"Icarus," again he cried aloud; his feathers he beheld in the waves. The dry land covers his bones; the sea retains his name.

Minos could not restrain the wings of a mortal; I myself am attempting to arrest a winged Divinity. If any one has recourse to the Hæmonian arts, and gives that which he has torn from the forehead of the young horse, 911 he is mistaken. The herbs of Medea will not cause love to endure; nor yet the Marsian spells 912 mingled with the magic notes. The Phasian damsel would have retained the son of Æson, Circe Ulysses, if love could only have been preserved through incantations. Philtres, too, causing paleness, 913 are of no use when administered to the fair. Philtres injure the intellect, and have a maddening effect. Afar be all criminal attempts; to be loved, be worthy to be loved; *a property* which comeliness, or beauty alone, will not confer upon you. Though you should be Nireus, 914 be praised by ancient Homer, and the charming Hylas, 915 carried off by the criminality of the Naiads; that you may retain your mistress, and not have to wonder that you are deserted, add the endowments of the mind to the advantages of the person. Beauty is a fleeting advantage; and the more it increases in years, the less it becomes, and, itself, is consumed by length of time.

Neither the violets nor the opening lilies bloom for ever; and, the roses lost, the thorny bush is prickly left behind. And, handsome man, soon shall come to you the hoary locks; soon shall come the wrinkles, to furrow your body over. Now form a disposition which may be lasting, and add it to your beauty; that alone endures to the closing pile. And be it no light care to cultivate the mind with the liberal arts, and to learn thoroughly the two languages, *the Latin and the Greek.* Ulysses was not handsome, but he was fluent; and yet with love he racked the ocean Goddesses. 916 Ah! how oft did Calypso grieve at his hastening to depart, and declare that the waves were not favorable to his oars! Again and again did she enquire into the catastrophe of Troy. Often in another manner was he wont to repeat the same thing. On the shore they were standing; even there did the beauteous Calypso enquire about the blood-stained death of the Odrysian chief.

With a little stick, for by chance he was holding a stick, he depicted on the firm shore the subject on which she was enquiring. "This is Troy," said he; and the walls he drew on the shore; "This must be Simois for thee, and suppose these to be my tents. There was a plain," and here he drew the plain, "which we moistened with the blood of Dolon, 917 while, as a spy, he was longing for the Hæmonian horses. 918 There were the tents of the Sithonian Rhesus; in this direction was I borne back again by the captured steeds." And many other things was he depicting, when the waves suddenly carried off both Pergamus and the tents of Rhesus together with their chief. Then the Goddess said, "Dost thou behold how famous names these waves have swept away, which thou dost trust will be favorable to thee about to depart?"

Come then, with hesitation, feel confidence in beauty so deceiving, whoever you are; or else possess something of more value than comeliness. A beseeming courtesy especially enlists the feelings; rudeness and harsh language promote hatred. We dislike the hawk, because it is always living in warfare; the wolves too, that are wont to rush upon the startled flocks. But the swallow, because it is gentle, is exempt from the snares of men; and the Chaonian bird 919 has the turrets for it to inhabit.

Afar lie all strife and contentions of the abusive tongue; with sweet words must gentle love be cherished. With strife let both wives persecute their husbands, and husbands their wives; and, each in their turn, let them ever be thinking that they must resort to law. 920 This is the part of wives; strife is the dowry of the wife. Let the mistress ever hear the accents that she longs for. At the bidding of no law have you come to live together; in your case 'tis love that performs the duties of the law. Bring soft caresses, and words that delight the ear, that she may *ever* be joyous at your approach.

I do not come as the instructor of the wealthy in Love; he who makes presents has no need of my experience. He who says, whenever he pleases, "Accept this," has a genius of his own. To him do I yield: he has greater attractions than have any discoveries of mine. I am the instructor of the poor, because, as a poor man, I have been in love. When I could not give presents, I gave verses. 921 Let the poor man love with caution, let the poor man stand in fear of bad language, and let him *put up with many a thing, not to be endured by the rich.*

I remember that once, when in a rage, I disarranged the hair of my mistress; of how many a day did that anger deprive me! I do not think I did, and I did not see that I had, torn her tunic, but she said so, and at my cost it was replaced. But you who are wise, avoid the errors of your instructor; and stand in awe of the punishment of my transgressions.

Let battles be with the Parthians, but be there peace with your refined mistress; mirth too, and whatever besides contains a reason for love. If she is not sufficiently kind or affable to you her lover; have patience, and bear it; after a time she will be softened. By giving way the supple branch is bent from the tree; if you make trial of your strength, you break it. By giving way the waves are swam across; but you cannot overcome the stream if you swim *against the flood* which the tide carries down. 'Tis yielding that subdues the tigers and the Numidian lions. By degrees only does the bull submit to the rustic plough. What was there more coy than Atalanta of Nonacris? 922 Yet, untamed as she was, she yielded to the deserving qualities of a man. They say that many a time, beneath the trees, Milanion wept at his mishaps, and the unkind conduct of the fair one. Full oft on his neck, as ordered, did he bear the treacherous toils; full oft with his cruel spear did he transfix the savage boars. Wounded, too, he experienced the stretched bow of Hylæus; 923 but yet there was another bow still more felt than this.

I do not bid you, in arms, to climb the woods of Mænalus, and I do not bid you to carry the toils upon your neck. Nor yet do I bid you to expose your breast to the discharged arrows. The requirements of my skill will be but light to the careful man. Yield to her when opposing; by yielding, you will come off victorious. Only take care to perform the part which she shall bid you. What she blames, do you blame; whatever she approves, do you approve; what she says, do you say; what she denies, do you deny. Does she smile, do you smile; if she weeps, do you remember to weep. Let her prescribe the law for the regulation of your features. If she plays, and throws the ivory cubes 924 with her hand, do you throw unsuccessfully, do you make bad moves 925 to the throws; or if you are throwing 926 the dice, let not the penalty attend upon her losing; take care that losing throws often befall yourself, if your piece is moving at the game that imitates 927 the tactics of war, take care that your man falls before his enemy of glass. Do you yourself hold the screen 928 stretched out by its ribs; do you make room in the crowd the way that she is going. And do not delay to place the footstool before the tasteful, couch; 929 and take off or put on the sandals for her delicate feet. Often, too, must the hand of your mistress, when cold, be made warm in your bosom, though you yourself should shiver in consequence. And think it no disgrace (although it should be a disgrace to you, still it will give pleasure), to hold the looking-glass 930 with the hand of a free-born man.

He who, by killing the monsters of his wearied step-mother, earned those heavens which before he had supported, is believed, amid the Ionian girls, to have held the work-basket, 931 and to have wrought the rough wool. The Tirynthian hero was obedient to the commands of his mistress. Go then, and hesitate to endure what he submitted to. When bidden to come to the Forum, take care always to be there before the appointed time; and do not go away until a late hour. Does she appoint to meet you at any place; put off everything else: run quickly, and let not the crowd stop your purposed route. Is she returning home at night, after having been at a feast; then, too, if she calls, come to her as though a servant. 932 If you are in the country and she says, "Come," (love hates the tardy) if a vehicle 933 is not at hand, go your journey on foot. Let neither bad weather nor the parching Dog-star detain you, nor the road made white with the snow that lies there.

Love is a kind of warfare; cowards, avaunt! These are not the standards to be defended by timid men. In this tender warfare, night, and wintry storms, and long journies, and cruel pain, and every kind of toil, have their part. Many a time will you have to endure the rain pouring from the clouds of heaven; cold and on the bare ground full oft will you lie. Cynthius 934 said to have fed the cows of Admetus of Pheræ, and to have lived in an humble cottage. What was becoming to Phoebus, to whom is it not becoming? Away with all conceit, whoever you are, who have a care for a lasting passion. If access is denied you by a safe and smooth path; and if her door shall be fastened by the bar put up; then, do you slip straight down through the open roof 935 let the high window, 936 too, present a secret passage. She will be pleased when she knows that she has proved the cause of risk to you. This will be to your mistress a pledge of your unvarying love. Full oft, Leander, couldst thou have done without thy mistress; that she might know thy passion, thou didst swim across.

And be not ashamed to make her handmaids, as each one is superior in rank, nor yet her male servants, entirely your own. Salute them each by name, there will be nothing thrown away: press their humble hands, proud lover, with your own. Moreover, (the expense is but trifling) give to the servant who asks, some little present from your means. Make a present, too, to the handmaid, on the day on which 937 the Gallic army, deceived by the garments of the matrons, received retribution. Follow my advice, and make the lower classes 938 your own; in that number let there always be the porter, and him who lies before the door of her chamber. And I do not bid you present to your mistress any costly gift; give her moderate ones, but, in your discrimination, well selected from those that are moderate. While the country is abundantly rich in produce, while the branches are bending beneath their load, let the boy bring your gifts from the country in his basket. You may say that they have been sent by you from your suburban retreat, although they may have been bought even in the Sacred Street. 939 Let him carry either grapes, or what Amaryllis was so fond of; 940 but, at the present day, she is fond of chesnuts no longer. And, besides, both with a thrush and a pigeon, 941 sent as a present, you may show how attentive you are to your mistress. By these means 942 are the expectations of death, and solitary old age, disgracefully made matter of purchase. Oh! may they perish through whom gifts promote criminal objects!

Why should I recommend you to send tender lines as well? Alas! poetry does not 943 gain much honour. Verses are praised: but 'tis costly gifts that are sought. If he is only rich, 944 a very barbarian is pleasing. Truly is this the golden age; the greatest honours accrue through gold; love is purchased with gold. Though thou thyself, Homer, shouldst come, attended by the Muses; if thou shouldst bring nothing with thee, thou wouldst be turned out of doors.

And yet there are the learned fair, a very limited number; another set are not learned, but they wish to be so. Both kinds may be praised in verse; the reader may set off the lines of whatever quality by a melodious voice. Indeed, a poem, carefully composed in their honour, will be to these or to those, as good, perhaps, as a little present. But take care that whatever you are about to do of your own accord and consider convenient, your mistress shall always first ask that of you. Has freedom been promised to any one of your slaves; still cause him to make a request for it of your mistress. If you forgive punishment and cruel fetters to your slave, let her be indebted to you for what you were about to do. Let the advantage be your own; let the credit be given to your mistress. Suffer no loss yourself, and let her act the part of the person in power.

But whosoever you are who have a care to retain the fair, cause her to believe that you are enchanted with her beauty. If she is in Tyrian costume, praise the dress of Tyrian hue; 945 if she is in that of Cos, 946 consider the Coan habit as becoming. Is she arrayed in gold, let her be more precious in your eyes than gold itself: if she wears a dress of felt, 947 praise the felt dress that she wears. Does she stand before you in her tunic, exclaim, "You are setting me on fire;" 948 but entreat her, with a voice of anxiety, to beware of the cold. Is the parting of her hair nicely arranged; praise the parting of it; has she curled her hair by aid of the fire: curled locks, do you prove the attraction. As she dances, admire her arms, her voice as she sings; and use the words of one complaining because she has left off. Her very embraces 949 you may commend, on the points that please yourself; and with murmuring accents you may signify your delight. Though she be more fierce than the grim Medusa; to her lover she will become gentle and kind.

Only, take you care that you be not discovered to be a deceiver in these expressions; and by your looks do not contradict your words. If devices are concealed, they are of use; when discovered, they cause shame, and deservedly remove confidence for all future time. Often, at the approach of autumn (when the year is most beauteous, and the filled grape is growing red with its purple juice; at the time when at one moment we are chilled with cold, at another we are melted with heat), through the varying temperature a languor takes possession of the body. She, indeed, may be in good health;

but if, through illness she keeps her bed, and, ailing, feels the bad effects of the weather, then let your love and affection be proved to the fair; then sow, that hereafter with the sickle of abundance you may reap. Let no disgust at her malady, that renders her so cross, come upon you: by your hands too, let whatever she will permit, be done. And let her see you as you weep; and be not tired of giving her kisses; and with her parched lips let her dry up your tears. Make many a vow for her cure, but all before her: and as often as she will permit, be seeing pleasant visions to tell her of. Let the old woman come, 950 too, to purify her couch and chamber; and in her palsied hand let her carry before her the sulphur and the eggs. In all these things there will be traces of a pleasing attention; for many a one has this road proved a path to another man's will. But still, let not loathing on the part of the sick fair be the result of your officiousness; let there be certain limits shown in your careful attentiveness. Do not you forbid her food, nor administer the cups with the bitter draught; let your rival mingle those.

But when you have gained the open sea, you must not use the breeze to which you set your sails from off the shore. While Love is wandering in his youth, let him gain strength by habit; if you nurse him well, in time he will be strong. Him that you fear as a bull, as a calf you were wont to pat; the tree under which you are now reclining, was once a twig. A river at its rise is small, but it acquires strength in its course; and where it runs, it now receives many a stream. Make her become used to you; there is nothing more powerful than habit. While you are courting her, avoid no amount of trouble. Let her be always seeing you; let her be always lending ear to you; let both night and day show your countenance. When you have a greater confidence that you may be missed; then, destined to be her care when absent, go away to a distance. Give yourself some repose; the land that has lain fallow, gives back in abundance what has been entrusted to it; and the dry ground sucks up the water of the heavens. Demophoôn, when present, inflamed Phyllis in a less degree; when he had set sail, more violently did she burn. The crafty Ulysses, by his absence, tortured Penelope: far away, tearful Laodamia, was thy hero of Phylace.

But a short respite alone is safe; in time, cares become modified, and the absent love decays and a new one makes its entrance. While Menelaus was absent, Helen, that she might not lie alone, was received at night into the warm bosom of his guest. What meant, Menelaus, this stupidity of thine? Thou didst go away alone; under the same roof were both the stranger and thy wife. And dost thou entrust, madman, the timid doves to the hawk? Dost thou entrust the well-filled sheep-fold to the mountain wolf? Helen commits no sin; this paramour of hers does no wrong; he does what thou, what any one, would do. Thou dost persuade them to adultery, by giving both time and opportunity. What advice, but thine own, has the fair made use of? What is she to do? Her husband is away, and a guest, no repulsive person, is present, and she is afraid to sleep alone in an empty couch. Let the son of Atreus think better of it: I acquit Helen of criminality; she made use of the opportunity given by an easy husband.

But neither is the tawny boar so fierce in the midst of his rage, when he hurls the furious dogs with the lightning shock of his tusks; nor the lioness, when she is giving the breast to her sucking whelps; nor the little viper, when inhired by the heedless foot; as the woman, who is furious on detecting the rival of her nuptial couch, and bears on her features the proofs of her feelings. To the sword and to flames does she resort; and, shame laid aside, onward she is impelled, as though struck by the horns of the Aonian God. The barbarian fair one of Phasis avenged the fault of her husband, and the violated rights of a wife, by the death of her sons. See, how another cruel parent ('tis the swallow that you behold) has her breast stained with blood. 'Tis this breaks those attachments that are firmly united, this, those of long duration; these faults must then be guarded against by cautious men.

But still, my judgment does not condemn you to one fair alone. The Gods forbid! hardly can the married woman adhere to this. Disport yourself; but let your faultiness be concealed by a decent stealthiness. No glory must be sought in one's own delinquency. And do you give no present of which the other may know; nor be there any stated times for your intriguing. And, lest the fair one should catch you in the retreat so well known to her, all must not be met in the same place of rendezvous. And, as often as you shall be writing, do you first examine the whole of the tablet; many a woman reads more than what has been sent to her. A slighted passion brandishes the arms of retribution, and hurls back the weapon, and causes yourself to complain of that of which it complained so lately.

So long as the son of Atreus was content with one woman, she, too, was chaste; through the fault of her husband did she become culpable. She had heard how that Chryses, bearing in his hand the laurel and the fillets, had not prevailed in behalf of his daughter. She had heard, too, ravished one of Lyrnesus, of thy sorrows; and how the warfare had been protracted through disgraceful delays. Still, these things she had only heard of; the daughter of Priam, herself, she had seen. Thou, the conqueror, wast the disgraced captive of thy own captive. Then did she receive the son of Thyestes, both into her chamber and her affections; and the daughter of Tyndarus avenged herself on a husband so deeply criminal.

Your actions, which you have studiously concealed, if perchance any of them are discovered, although they should be notorious, still do you always deny them. On such occasions, do you neither be subdued, nor more kind than usual. That bears the marks of a mind that has too deeply offended. Still, spare not any endearments on your side; peace is entirely centred in caresses alone; by these must the former intrigue be disavowed. There are some who would recommend you to use injurious herbs, such as savory; in my opinion they are so many poisons. Or else, they mingle pepper with the seed of the stinging nettle; 952 and the yellow camomile pounded in old wine. But the Goddess, whom the lofty Eryx receives beneath his shady hill, does not allow us to be impelled in such manner to her delights. The white onion 953 which is sent from the Pelasgian city of Alcathoiis, 954 and the salacious herbs which come out of the gardens, and eggs may be eaten; the honey of Hymettus may be eaten, and the nuts which the pine-tree with its sharp leaves produces.

Why, learned Erato, art thou thus diverging into the medical art? The inner side of the turning-place must be grazed by my chariot. You, who just now were, by my recommendation, to conceal your delinquencies, change your course, and, by my advice, disclose your intrigues. Nor yet is any inconsistency of mine to be censured; the curving ship does not always carry those on board with the same breezes. For sometimes we run with the Thracian Boreas, sometimes with the East wind; full aft does the canvass swell with the Zephyrs, with the South wind full aft. See how, in the chariot, the driver, at one moment, gives the flowing rein, at another, skilfully checks the horses in full career. There are some, with whom an anxious obsequiousness is ruinous, and if there is no rival existing, then their passion waxes faint. The feelings often run riot amid prosperity; and to bear good fortune with equanimity is no easy task. As the declining fire, its strength consuming by degrees, itself lies concealed, and the ashes become white over the surface of the fire; but still, when sulphur is applied, it finds the flames that were extinguished, and the light returns which existed before; so, when the feelings, sluggish through repose, and free from care, become torpid, by sharp stimulants must love be aroused. Make her to be jealous on your account, and rekindle her deadened feelings; let her turn pale at the proof of your inconstancy.

Oh four times blest, and so oft, that it is not possible to limit it to numbers, is that man, on whose account the slighted fair is in grief! who, soon as the charge has reached her unwilling ears, faints away: and both her voice and colour leave the sorrowing fair. Would that I were he, whose locks she tears in her fury; would that I were he, whose tender cheeks she tears with her nails; whom she looks upon bursting into tears; whom she beholds with scowling eyes; without whom she cannot exist; *but still* wishes that she could. If you enquire as to its duration: let the time be short for her to complain of her injuries, lest her anger may acquire strength in the slowly passing lapse of time.

And now let her fair neck be encircled in your arms; and as she weeps, she must be received in your bosom. Give her kisses as she weeps: bestow her caresses as she weeps. Peace will ensue: by this method alone is anger appeased. When she has been passionately raving, when she shall seem to be an assured enemy; then seek your treaty of peace in caresses; she will then be pacified. For 'tis there that Concord dwells, all arms laid aside; 'tis in that spot, believe me, that the Graces were born. The doves which fought the moment before, are now billing; their cooing has the meaning of caresses, and of words.

At first 955 there was a confused mass of things without arrangement; and the stars, the earth, and the ocean, were but of one appearance. Afterwards, the heavens were placed above the earth; the land was surrounded by the sea, and the confused Chaos was divided into its elements. The woods received the beasts, the air the birds as its possession; in the flowing waters, you, fishes were concealed. At that time the human race wandered in the solitary woods: and it consisted of nothing but brute force, and a mind quite uninformed. The woods were their houses, grass their food, and leaves their beds; and for a long time the one was unknown to the other. Voluptuous pleasure is said to have been the first to soften their rude dispositions; afterwards, the woman and the man settled in the same spot. What should they do?

They had been instructed by no preceptor: Venus completed this delightful task without any art. The bird has an object to love: the female fish finds in the midst of the waters an object with which to share her joys. The hind follows her mate; the serpent couples with the serpent; the bitch, too, consorts with the dog. The delighted sheep unites with the ram; the heifer, also, is pleased with the bull; the fiat-nosed she-goat, too, receives her unclean mate. 956 Mares are driven to frenzy, and follow the horses, separated by streams, over places far distant from each other in situation. Come, then, and give an efficacious remedy to the angered fair; 'tis that alone that puts an end to violent grief. 'Tis that remedy which excels the potions of Machaon; 957 through that, when you have offended, you will have to be reinstated.

While I was thus singing, Apollo, suddenly appearing, touched with his thumb the strings of his lyre inlaid with gold. In his hands there was a laurel, placed on his holy locks there was a laurel: visible as a Poet he came. 958 "Thou instructor in wanton Love," says he, "come, lead thy pupils to my temples. There is there a sentence celebrated in fame over the universal world, which bids each one to know himself. 959 He who shall be known to himself, will alone love with prudence, and will proportion every task to his strength. He to whom nature has given beauty, for that let him be admired; he who has a fair complexion, let him often lie down with a shoulder exposed. He who charms with his discourse, let him break the quietude of silence; he who sings with skill, let him sing; he who drinks with elegance, 960 let him drink. But in the middle of a conversation, neither let those who are eloquent declaim, and let not the insane poet be reciting his own compositions."

Thus Phoebus recommended; observe this recommendation of Phoebus. There is full confidence in the hallowed lips of this Divinity. I am now called to my more immediate subject: whoever shall love with prudence, he will prove successful, and will obtain from my skill what he shall require. The furrows do not always return with interest that which has been entrusted to them; nor does the breeze always aid the veering barks. What pleases lovers, is but a little: 'tis much more that crosses them; let them resolve to endure many things with their feelings. As many as are the hares on Athos; 961 as the bees that feed on Hybla; 962 as the berries which the azure-coloured tree of Pallas bears; as the shells on the sea-shore; so many are the pangs of love; the shafts which we endure are reeking with plenteous gall.

She, whom perchance you shall see, will be said to have gone out of doors; believe that she is gone out of doors, and that you make a mistake in your seeing. Is the door shut against you on the appointed night; endure even to lay your body on the dirty ground. Perhaps, too, the lying maid will say with a haughty air, "Why is that fellow blocking up our door?" Suppliantly entreat even the door-posts of the obdurate fair; and place at the door the roses that have been taken from off your head. 963 Come when she desires it; when she shall shun you, you'll go away. It is not becoming for men of good breeding to cause weariness of their company. Why should your mistress be able to say of you, "There is no getting rid of this man?" The senses 964 are not on the alert at all hours. And deem it no disgrace to put up with the curses of the fair one, or her blows, nor yet to give kisses to her delicate feet.

But why dwell upon trifles? Let my mind be occupied with greater subjects. Of great matters will I sing; people, give all attention. I attempt an arduous task, but merit there is none, but what is secured by arduous means. By my undertaking are laborious attempts required. Endure a rival with patience; the victory will rest with yourself; you will be the conqueror on the heights of mighty Jove. 965 Believe that not a mortal tells you this, but the Pelasgian oaks of Dodona: my skill has nothing superior to this to teach you. Does she make a sign to him, do you put up with it; does she write, don't you touch the tablets; let her come from whatever place she likes; and wherever she chooses, let her go. This do husbands allow to their lawful wives; even, too, when thou, gentle sleep, 966 dost come to thy duty. I confess, that in this art I myself am not yet perfect. What must I do? I am myself unequal to my own precepts. And is any one in my presence to be making signs to my mistress? And am I to endure it? And is not my anger to hurry me away to any extreme? Her own husband 967 (I remember it well) gave her a kiss; I complained of kisses being given; my love is brimful of fierceness. Not once alone has this failing proved an injury to me; he is more skilful, by whose encouragement other men visit 968 his mistress. But 'tis still better to know nothing of it. Allow stealthy intrigues to lie concealed, lest the blush of confession should fly in future from her countenance when detected.

With greater reason then, ye youths, forbear to detect your mistresses. Let them be guilty; and guilty, let them suppose that they have deceived you. When detected, the passion increases; when the fortune of the two is the same, each persists in the cause of the disgrace. There is a story told, very well known in all the heavens, how Mars and Venus 969 were caught by the contrivance of Mulciber. Father Mars, distracted by a frantic passion for Venus, from a terrible warrior, became a lover. Neither did Venus (for, indeed, no Goddess is there more kind) proved coy or stubborn to Gradivus. O how many a time is she said, in her wantonness, to have laughed at the feet of her husband, and at his hands, hardened with the fire or his handicraft. In the presence of Mars, mocking him, she imitated her husband, and she was beauteous *even while so doing*; and many a grace was there combined with her charms. But they were in the habit of skilfully concealing their early intercourse; and their frailty was replete with modest propriety. Through the information of the Sun (who is there that can deceive the Sun?), the actions of his wife became known to Vulcan. Thou Sun, what a bad example thou art setting! Ask a bribe of her; and shouldst thou hold thy tongue, she has a favour which she may grant to thee.

Around and above the bed, Muleiber disposes the hidden toils; the work, by its fineness, escapes their eyes. He pretends a journey to Lemnos; the lovers come, according to the appointment; entangled in the toils, they both lie naked. He calls the Gods together; the captives afford a spectacle. People believe that Venus could hardly restrain her tears. They cannot conceal their faces; they cannot, in fact, veil their modesty with their hands. Upon this, one says, laughing, 970 "Transfer to me thy chains, most valiant Mavors, if they are a burden to thee." With difficulty, Neptune, at thy entreaty, does he release their captured bodies. Mars makes for Thrace, 971 and she for Paphos. 972 This, Vulcan, was done by thee; what before they used to conceal, they now do more openly, since all modesty is gone. Yet often, foolish one, dost thou confess that thou didst act unwisely; and they say that thou hast repented of thy wrath. This I have already forbidden: lo! Dione forbids you to suffer that detection which she herself endured. And do you arrange no toils for your rival; and intercept no words written by the hand in secret. Let the men seek for those, (if, indeed, they think they ought to be sought for) whom the fire and water render 973 lawful husbands.

Behold! again do I protest; no sportive subject is here treated of, but what is permitted by the laws; there is no matron concerned with my sallies. 974 Who would dare to publish to the profane the rites of Ceres, 975 and the great mysteries that were established in the Thracian Samos? 'Tis a small merit to hold one's silence upon matters; but, on the other hand, 'tis a grievous fault to speak of things on which we should be silent. O justly does it happen, that the blabbing Tantalus is thirsting in the midst of the water, the apples on the tree being caught at by him in vain! Cytherea especially bids her rites to be concealed. I recommend no talkative person to approach them.

If the mysteries of Venus are not enclosed in chests, 976 and the hollow cymbals do not resound with frantic blows; although among ourselves they are celebrated by universal custom, yet it is in such a manner that among us they demand concealment. Venus herself, as oft as she lays her garments aside, conceals her groin with the left hand, 977 a little bent back. The cattle couple in public and promiscuously; even when this is seen, full oft the fair one turns away her face. Chambers and doors are provided for our stealthy dalliance; and our nakedness lies concealed by garments placed over it. And if we do not require darkness, still we do something of a retired shade, and something less exposed than open day. In those times, even, when tiles did not as yet keep out the sun and the shower, but the oak was affording both shelter and food; in the groves and caves, and not in the open air, were shared the delights of love. So great was the regard for modesty, even in a savage race. But now-a-days we give praises to the exploits of the night; and nothing beyond the power of talking of it, is purchased at a heavy price. 978 You will, for sooth, be discussing all the damsels in every quarter, that you may say to every person, "She, too, has been mine," that none may be wanting for you to point at with your fingers; and as you touch upon each, there will be a scandalous tale. But I am complaining of trifles; some pretend things, which, if true, they would deny, and not declare that there is not a woman from whom they have not received the last favour. If they cannot meddle with their persons, so far as they can, they meddle with their names; and, their persons untouched, their reputation bears the blame.

Go now, odious keeper, and shut the doors of the fair: and add to the solid door-posts a hundred bars. What safety is there, while the defiler of character exists, and desires to be thought that he is that which it has not proved his lot to be? Even my real amours I confess but with reserve, and my secret intrigues are concealed with sure fidelity. Especially forbear to censure the blemishes of the fair; to many it has proved of advantage to conceal them. Her complexion was not made an objection against Andromeda by him, on whose two feet were the waving wings. 979 To all others Andromache seemed of larger stature 980 than was becoming; Hector was the only one who called her of moderate size. What you endure with impatience, accustom yourself to; and you will endure it with patience. Length of time makes many things endurable; but a rising passion catches sight of everything. While the young branch is uniting within the green bark, 981 whatever breeze shakes it while now tender, it falls. Soon, hardened in time, the same tree will stoutly resist the winds, and bear the adopted fruit.

Time itself removes all blemishes from the person; and what was a fault, in lapse of time ceases so to be. The nostrils that are unaccustomed to it, are not able to endure the hides of bulls; the odour is not perceived by those that have been rendered used to it in length of time. We may palliate faults by names; let her be called swarthy, whose blood is blacker than the pitch of Illyria. If she has a cast in the eyes, she is like Venus: if yellow haired, like Minerva. She that is only half alive through her leanness, let her be grace ful. Whatever woman is small, say that she is active; her that is gross, call plump; and let each fault lie concealed in its proximity to some good quality.

And don't you enquire what year she is now passing, nor under what Consulship 982 she was born; a privilege which the rigid Censor 983 possesses. And this, especially, if she has passed the bloom of youth, and her best years 984 are fled, and she now pulls out the whitening hairs. This age, O youths, or even one more advanced, has its advantages; this soil will produce its crops, this is worth the sowing. While strength and years permit, endure labour; soon will bending old age come with silent foot. Either cleave the ocean with the oars, or the earth with the plough; or turn your warlike hands to cruel arms; or devote your strength and your attention to the fair. This, too, is a kind of warfare; 985 this, too, seeks its advantages. Besides, in these 986 there is a greater acquaintance with their subject; and there is long practice, which alone renders skilful. By attention to dress they repair the ravages of years; and by carefulness they cause themselves not to appear aged.

Utque velis, Venerem jungunt per mille figuras.
Inveniat plures nulla tabella modos.

Illis sentitur non irritata voluptas:

Quod juvet, ex æquo fœmina virque ferant.

Odi concubitus, qui non utrumque resolvunt;

Hoc est, cur pueri tangar amore minus.

Odi quæ præbet, quia sit præbere necesse;

Siccaque de lanâ cogitât ipsa suâ.

Quæ datur officio, non est mihi grata voluptas,

Officium faciat nulla puella mihi.

Me voces audire juvat sua gaudia fassas:

Utque morer memet, sustineamque roget.

Aspiciam dominse victos amends ocellos.

Langueat; et tangi se vetet ilia diu.

Those advantages has nature given not to early youth, which are wont to spring up soon after seven times five years 987 have passed. Those who are in a hurry, let them drink of new wine; for me let the cask, stored up in the times 988 of ancient Consuls, pour forth the wine of my ancestors. No plane-tree but a mature one is able to withstand Phoebus; the shooting grass, 989 too, hurts the tender feet. And could you, forsooth, have preferred Hermione 990 to Helen? And was Gorge 991 more attractive than her mother? Whoever you are that wish to enjoy matured passion, if you only persevere, you will obtain a fitting reward.

Conscius ecce duos accepit lectus amantes:

Ad thalami clausas, Musa, résisté fores.

Sponte suâ, sine te, celoberrima verba loquentur:

Nec manus in lecto læva jacebit iners.

Invenient digiti, quod agant in partibus illis,

In quibus occulte spicula figit Amor.

Fecit in Andromache prius hoc fortissimus Hector;

Nec solum bellis utüis file fuit.

Fecit et in captâ Lyrneside magnus Achilles,

Cum premeret mollem lassus ab hoste torum.

Illis, te tangi manibus, Brisei, sinebas,

Imbutæ Phrygiâ quæ nece semper erant.

An fuit hoc ipsum, quod te lasciva juvaret

Ad tua victrices membra venire manus?

Crede mihi, non est Yeneris properanda voluptas:

Sed sensim tarda prolicienda morâ.

Cum loca repereris, quæ tangi fœmina gaudet;

Non obstet, tangas quo minus ilia, pudor.

Adspicics oculos tremulo fulgore micantes,

Ut sol a liquida sæpe refulget aquâ.

Accèdent questus, accedet amabile murmur,

Et dulces gemitus, aptaque verba loco.

Sed neque tu dominam velis majoribus usus

Desine; nec cursus anteat ilia tuos.

Ad metam properate simul; turn plena voluptas,

Cum pariter victi foemina virque jacent.

Hi tibi servandus tenor est, cum libera dantur

Otia; furtivum nec timor urget opus.

Cum mora non tuta est, totis incumbere remis

Utile, et admisso subdere calcar equo.

There is an end now of my task; grant me the palm, ye grateful youths, and present the myrtle garlands to my perfumed locks. As great as was Podalirius 992 among the Greeks in the art of healing, as the descendant of Æacus with his right hand, as Nestor with his eloquence; as great as Calchas 993 was in soothsaying, as the son of Telamon was in arms, as Automedon 994 was in guiding the chariot, so great a Lover am I. Celebrate me as your bard, ye men, to me repeat my praises; let my name be sung throughout all the earth. Arms have I given to you; to Achilles Vulcan gave arms. With the gifts presented to you, prove victorious, as he proved victorious. But whoever subdues the Amazon with my weapons, let him inscribe upon his spoil 995 —"Naso was my preceptor."

And lo! the charming fair are asking me to give them my precepts. You then shall be the next care of my song.— —

BOOK- THE THIRD.

With arms against the Amazons I have furnished the Greeks. Arms remain for me to present, Penthesilea, 1001 to thee and to thy squadrons. Go to the combat equally prepared; and may those prove the victors, whom genial Dione 1002 favours, and the Boy who flies over the whole world. It was not fair for the females unprotected to engage with the men in arms, and so it would have been disgraceful for you to conquer, ye men.

One of the multitude may say, "Why add venom to the serpent? And why deliver the sheep-fold to the ravening wolf? Forbear to lay the culpability of the few upon the many; and let each fair one be considered according to her own deserts. If the younger son of Atreus has Helen, and the elder son of Atreus 1003 has the sister of Helen, to charge with criminality, if the son of Oclus, 1004 through the wickedness of Eriphyle, daughter of Talaion, alive, and with living steeds, descended to Styx; there is Penelope constant, while her husband was wandering for twice five years, and for as many years engaged in war. Witness the hero from Phylace, 1005 and her who is said to have descended as the companion of her husband, and to have died before her destined years. The wife from Pagasæ redeemed the son of Pheres 1006 from death, and in place of 1007 the funeral of her husband, the wife was carried out. "Receive me, Capaneus; we will mingle our ashes," said the daughter of Iphis, and she leapt on the midst of the pile. Virtue, herself, too, is a female, both in dress and name. 'Tis not to be wondered at, if she favours her own sex.

But still, 'tis not such dispositions as these that are required by my art. Sails of less magnitude are befitting my skiff. 1008 Nothing but wanton dalliance is taught by me; in what manner a woman is to be loved, I purpose to teach. The woman repels neither the flames, nor the cruel bow; those weapons, I see, make less havoc among the men. Many a time do the men prove false; not often the charming fair; and, if you make inquiry, they have but few charges of fraud against them. Jason, the deceiver, repudiated the Phasian, when now a mother; and into the bosom of the son of Æson there came another bride. 1009 Ariadne, left alone in an unknown spot, had fed the sea-birds, so far, Theseus, as thou wast concerned. Enquire why she is said to have gone on her nine journeys, 1010 and hear how the woods lamented Phyllis, their foliage laid aside. And Elissa, she has the credit of affection; and still, that guest of thine, Elissa, afforded both the sword and the cause for thy destruction. Shall I tell what it was that ruined thee? Thou didst not know how to love; thou wast wanting in skill; through skill, love flourishes for ever.

Even still would they have been ignorant, but Cytherea commanded me to instruct them, and stood, herself, before my eyes. Then to me she said, "Why have the unfortunate fair deserved this? An unarmed multitude is handed over to the men in arms. Two treatises 1011 have rendered them skilful; this side, as well, must be instructed by thy advice. He who before had uttered 1012 reproaches against the wife from Therapnæ, soon sang her praises to a more fortunate lyre. If well I know thee, injure not the fair whom thou dost adore; their favour must be sought by thee so long as thou shalt live."

Thus she said; and from the myrtle (for she was standing with her locks wreathed with myrtle) she gave me a leaf and a few berries. Receiving them, I was sensible of the divine influence as well; the sky shone with greater brightness, and all care departed from my breast. While she inspires my genius; hence receive the precepts, ye fair, which propriety, and the laws, and your own privileges, 1013 allow you. Even now, be mindful of old age, that one day will come; then will no time be passed by you in idleness. Disport yourselves, while yet you may, and while even now you confess to your true years; after the manner of the flowing stream, do the years pass by. Neither shall the water which has past by, be ever recalled; nor can the hour which has past, ever return. You must employ your youthful age; with swift step age is gliding on; and that which follows, is not so pleasing as that which having passed was charming. Those brakes, which are withering, I have beheld as beds of violets; from amid those brambles, has a beauteous chaplet been gathered for myself.

The time will be, when you, who are now shutting out a lover, will be lying, an old woman, chilled in the lonely night. No door 1014 of yours will be broken open in the broils of the night; nor will you find in the morning your threshold bestrewed with roses. 1015 How soon, ah me! are our bodies pursed with wrinkles, and that colour which existed in the beauteous face, fades away! The grey hairs, too, which you might have sworn that you had had from childhood, will suddenly be sprinkled over all your head. Old age is thrown off by serpents, together with the light slough; and the shedding of their horns makes the stags not to be old. Our advantages fly irretrievably; pluck the flowers then; if they be not plucked, they will lamentably fade themselves to your sorrow. Besides, child-bearing makes the hours of youth more short-lived; with continual crops the soil waxes old.

Endymion of Latmus, O Moon, causes not thee to blush; nor was Cephalus a prey for the rosy Goddess to be ashamed of. Though Adonis be allowed to Venus, whom she yet laments; whence had she Æneas and Hermione 1016 for her children? Follow, O race of mortals, the example of the Goddesses; and refuse not your endearments to the eager men. Even should they deceive you, what do you lose? All remains the same. Were a thousand to partake thereof, nothing is wasted thereby. Iron is worn away, stones are consumed by use; your persons are proof against all apprehension of detriment. Who would forbid light to be taken from another light presented? Or who, on the deep sea, would hoard up the expanse of waters? "But 'tis not right," you say, "for any woman to grant favours to a man." Tell me, what are you losing but the water, which you may take up again? 1017 Nor are my words urging you to prostitution; but they are forbidding you to fear evils that do not exist: your favours are exempt from loss to yourselves.

But while I am in harbour, let a gentle breeze impel me, destined to sail with the blasts of a stronger gale. I begin with dress: 1018 from the well-dressed vine Bacchus has birth; and in the well-dressed field the high corn springs up. Beauty is the gift of the Divinity; how many a one prides herself on her beauty? Still, a great part 1019 of you is wanting in such endowments. Care will confer charms; charms neglected will perish, even though she be like the Idalian Goddess. If the fair of olden times did not pay such attention to their persons; neither had the ancients men so well-dressed. If Andromache was clad in a coarse tunic, what wonder is it? She was the wife of a hardy soldier. And would his companion, forsooth, come bedecked to Ajax, him whose covering was seven hides of oxen. Formerly a rustic simplicity existed: now gorgeous Rome possesses the wealth of the subdued earth. See the Capitol, what it now is and what it was, you would declare that they belonged to different Jupiters. The Senate-house, which is now right worthy of an assemblage so august, when Tatius held the sway, was made of straw. The fields of the Palatine hill, which are now resplendent in honour of Phoebus 1020 and our rulers, what were they but pastures for the oxen that ploughed?

Let old times delight others: I congratulate myself that I am born thus late; this is the age that is suited to my tastes. Not because the pliable gold is now dug out of the earth, and choice shells 1021 come here from foreign shores; nor yet because, the marble cut out, mountains diminish; nor yet because the azure waves are kept out by the moles. 1022 But because civilization prevails; and because the rude manners that flourished with our ancient forefathers have not come down to our days.

But do not you as well load your ears with precious stones, which the tawny Indian seeks in the green waves. And do not go forth heavily loaded with clothes embroidered with gold: by the wealth through which you seek to attract us, you often drive us away. By neatness we are captivated; let not your hair be without arrangement; the hands applied to it both give beauty and deny it. The method, too, of adorning is not a single one; let each choose the one that is becoming it to her, and let her first consult her mirror. An oval face becomes a parting upon the unadorned head: Laodamia had her hair thus arranged. Round features 1023 require a little knot to be left for them on the top of the head, so that the ears may be exposed. Let the hair of another he thrown over either shoulder. In such guise art thou, tuneful Phoebus, thy lyre being assumed. Let another Lave her hair tied behind after the manner of well-girt Diana, as she is wont when she hunts the scared wild beasts. It becomes another to have her floating locks to flow loosely: another must be bound by fillets over her fastened tresses. Another it delights to be adorned with the figure of the tortoise 1024 of the Cyllenian God: let another keep up her curls that resemble the waves. 1025

But neither will you count the acorns on the branching native oak, nor how many bees there are in Hybla, nor how many wild beasts on the Alps: nor am I able to comprehend in numbers so many modes; *each successive day brings a new fashion.* Even neglected locks are becoming to many; often would you suppose that they are lying neglected since yesterday; the very moment before they have been combed afresh. Let art imitate chance. 'Twas thus that, in the captured city, when Hercules beheld Iole; "Her," said he, "do I love." In such guise, deserted fair one of Gnossus, did Bacchus bear thee away in his chariot, while the Satyrs shouted Evôe! O how indulgent is nature to your beauty, whose blemishes can be atoned for in fashions so numerous! We men, to our misfortune, become bald; and our hair, carried away by time, falls off, like Boreas shaking down the leaves.

The female stains her grey hair with the herbs from Germany; 1026 and by art a colour is sought superior to the genuine one. The female walks along, thickly covered with purchased hair; and for money 1027 she makes that of others—here comes those of fair complexion: black became the laughter of Brises.

Nor is she ashamed to buy it openly: we see it being sold before the eyes of Hercules 1028 and the Virgin throng.

What am I to say on clothing? Gold flounces, 1029 I have no need of you; nor you, the wool which dost blush twice dipt in Tyrian purple. Since so many colours can be procured at a lower price, what folly it is to be carrying a fortune on one's person. 1030 Lo! there is the colour of the sky, at the time when the sky is without clouds, and the warm South wind is not summoning the showers of rain. Lo! there is the colour like to thee, that art said 1031 once to have borne away Phryxus and Helle from the treachery of Ino. That which resembles the waves, 1032 has its name, too, from the waves; I could imagine that the Nymphs are clad in vestments of this colour. Another resembles saffron; in saffron-coloured garments is the dewy Goddess dressed, when she yokes her steeds that bear the light of day. Another resembles the Paphian myrtles; another the purple amethysts, or the white roses, or the Thracian crane. Neither are there wanting, Amaryllis, 1033 thy chesnuts, nor yet almonds; and wax 1034 has given its own name to woollen textures.

As many as the flowers which the renewed earth produces, when in warm spring the vine puts forth its buds, and sluggish winter retreats; so many, or still more, shades of dye does the wool imbibe. Choose them by rule; for every colour will not be suitable to every complexion.

When she was carried off, then, too, was she clothed in a dark garment. White befits the swarthy; in white, daughter of Cepheus, thou wast charming; by thee, thus clothed, was Seriphos 1035 trodden.

How nearly was I recommending you that there should be no shocking goat 1036 in the armpits, and that your legs should not be rough with harsh hair. But I am not instructing fair ones from the crags of Caucasus, and who are drinking, Mysian Caïcus, of thy waves. Besides; need I to recommend that idleness should not blacken your teeth, and that your mouth ought to be washed each morning with water used for the purpose. You know, too, how to find whiteness in an application of wax; 1037 she who is blushing with no real blood, is blushing by the aid of art. With skill do you fill up the bared edges of the eye-brows, 1038 and the little patch 1039 covers your cheeks in all their genuineness. 'Tis no harm, too, to mark the eyes 1040 slightly with ashes; or with saffron, produced, beauteous Cydnus, near to thee. I have a little treatise, 1041 but through the care bestowed, a great work, in which I have mentioned the various recipes for your beauty. From that as well, do you seek aid for your diminished charms: my skill is not idle in behalf of your interests.

But let not your lover discover the boxes exposed upon the table; art, by its concealment only, gives aid to beauty. Whom would not the paint disgust, besmeared all over your face, when, through its own weight, it flows and falls upon your heated bosom? Why is the smell of the oesypum 1042 so powerful, sent from Athens though it be, an extract drawn from the filthy fleece of the sheep? Nor would I recommend you in his presence to apply the mixture of the marrow of the deer, 1043 nor before him to clean your teeth. These things will give you good looks, but they will be unbecoming to be seen; there are many things, too, which, disgusting while being done, add charms when done. The statues which now bear the name of the laborious Myron, 1044 were once a sluggish weight and a solid mass. That the ring may be made, the gold is first beaten; the clothes, that you are wearing, were once dirty wool. While it was being wrought, it was hard stone; now, as a beautiful statue, 1045 naked Venus is wringing the moisture from her dripping locks.

You, too, while you are dressing, let us suppose to be asleep; after the finishing hand, you will be seen much more àpropos. Why is the cause of the fairness of your complexion known to me? Shut the door of your chamber, why expose the work half done? It is proper for the men to be in ignorance of many a thing. The greatest part of things would cause disgust, if you were not to conceal what is within. Examine the gilded statues which hang in the decorated theatre; how thin the tinsel that covers the wood. But it is not permitted the public to approach them unless completed; neither ought your charms to be heightened unless the men are at a distance. But I would not forbid you to allow your hair to be combed in their presence, so that it may be flowing along your back. Only take care especially on such occasions not to be cross; and do not many times undo your hair, pulled down, when fastened up. Let your coiffeuse be with a whole skin. I detest her who tears the face of her attendant with her nails, and who, seizing the hair-pin, pierces her arms. 1046 As she touches the head of her mistress, she curses it; and at the same time, streaming with blood, she is crying over the odious locks.

The fair one that has but little hair, let her set a watch on her threshold; or let her always make her toilet in the temple 1047 of the Good Goddess. I was unexpectedly announced as having paid a visit to a certain lady; in her confusion, she put on her locks the wrong side before. May a cause of shame so disgraceful fall to the lot of my foes, and may that dishonour happen to the Parthian dames. A mutilated animal is repulsive, the fields without grass are repulsive; and so is a shrub without foliage, and a head without hair. You have not come to be instructed by me, Semele, or Leda, thou, too, Sidonian fair, 1048 who wast borne across the sea upon the fictitious bull; or Helen, whom, Menelaus, not without reason, thou didst demand to be restored to thee, and whom, not without reason, thou Trojan ravisher, didst retain. A multitude comes to be instructed, both pretty and ugly damsels; and the unsightly are ever more in number than the good-looking. The beauteous care less for the resources and the precepts of art; they have their own endowments, charms that are powerful without art. When the sea is calm, the sailor rests free from care; when it becomes boisterous, he appeals to his own resources.

Few, however, are the forms free from defect. Conceal your blemishes; and, so far as you can, hide the imperfections of your person. If you are short, sit down; that, while standing, you may not appear to be sitting; and if of a diminutive size, throw yourself upon your couch. Here, too, that your measure may not be able to be taken as you lie, take care that your feet are concealed with the clothes 1049 thrown over them. She who is too thin, let her wear clothes of thick texture; and let her vestments hang loosely from her shoulders. Let her who is pale, tint her complexion with purple stripes; 1050 do you that are more swarthy, have recourse to the aid of the Pharian fish. 1051 Let an ill-shaped foot be always concealed in a boot of snow-white leather steeped in alum; and do not unloose their laced sandals from the spindly legs. For high shoulders, small pads are suitable; 1052 and let the girth 1053 encircle the bosom that is too prominent. She whose fingers are dumpy, and whose nails are rough, should mark with but little gesture whatever is said. She, whose breath is strong smelling, should never talk with an empty stomach; and she should always stand at a distance 1054 from her lover's face.

If your teeth are black, or large, or not, growing straight, you will suffer very great inconvenience from laughing. Who could have supposed it? The fair take lessons even in laughing; and even in that respect is gracefulness studied by them. Let your mouth be but moderately open; let the dimples on either side he but small; and let the extremity of the lips cover the upper part of the teeth. And do not let your sides be shaking with prolonged laughter; but let them utter sounds gentle and feminine, to I know not what degree. Some there are, who distort their face with an unsightly grin; another, when she is joyous in her laughter, you would take to be crying. Another makes a harsh noise, and screams in a disagreeable manner; just as the unsightly she-ass brays by the rough mill-stone.

To what point does not art proceed? Some study how to weep with grace, and cry at what time and in what manner they please. Nay, further; when the letters are deprived of their full sound, and the lisping tongue becomes contracted with an affected pronunciation; then is grace sought in an imperfection; to pronounce certain words badly, they learn to be less able to speak than they really are. To all these points, since they are of consequence, give attention. Learn how to walk with steps suited to a female. Even in the gait, there are certain points of gracefulness not to be disregarded; this both attracts and repels men who are strange to you. This fair one moves her sides with skill, and with her flowing tunics catches the breeze, and haughtily moves her extended feet. Another walks just like the redfaced spouse of some Umbrian 1055 husband, and, straddling, takes huge strides. But, as in many other things, let there be a medium here as well; one movement is clownish; another movement will be too mincing in its gait. But let the lower part of your shoulders, and the upper part of your arm be bare, to be beheld from your left hand upwards. This is especially becoming to you, ye of fair complexion; when I see this, I have always a longing to give a kiss to the shoulder, where it is exposed.

The Sirens were monsters of the deep, which with their tuneful voices detained the ships, even though in full career. On hearing them, the son of Sisyphus 1056 almost released his body from the mast; for the wax 1057 was melted in the ears of his companions. The voice is an insinuating quality; let the fair learn how to sing. In place of beauty, her voice has proved the recommendation of many a woman. And sometimes let them repeat what they have heard in the marble theatres; and sometimes the songs attuned to the measures of the Nile. 1058 Neither, in my way of thinking, ought a clever woman to be ignorant how to hold the plectrum 1059 in her right hand, the lyre in her left. Orpheus of Rhodope with his lyre moved rocks, and wild beasts, and the lakes of Tartarus, and Cerberus the triple dog. At thy singing, most righteous avenger of thy mother, 1060 the attentive stones built up the walls. The fish, (the well-known story of the lyre of Arion, 1061 although he was dumb, is supposed to have been moved by his voice. Learn, too, to sweep the chords of the festive psaltery 1062 with your two hands; 'tis an instrument suited to amorous lays.

Let the songs of Callimachus 1063 be known to you, let those of the poet of Cos, 1064 let the Teian Muse too, of the drunken old bard. Let Sappho, too, be well known; for what is there more exciting than she? Or than him, through whom 1065 the father is deceived by the tricks of the crafty Geta? You may, too, have read the poems of the tender Propertius, 1066 or something of Gallus, or thy works, Tibullus. 1067 The fleece, too, so bewailed, O Phryxus, of thy sister, shining with its yellow hair, celebrated by Varro. 1068 The exiled Æneas, as well, the first origin of lofty Rome, 1069 than which no work exists in Latium of greater fame.

Perhaps, too, my name will be mingled among these, and my writings will not be consigned to the waters of Lethe. And people will one day say, "Read the elegant lines of our master, in which he instructs the two sides. 1070 Or of his three books, which the title designates as, 'The Amours,' choose a portion to read with skilful lips, in a languishing way. Or let his Epistles be repeated by you with well-modulated voice; this kind of composition, 1071 unknown to others, did he invent." O Phoebus, mayst thou so will it; so too, ye benignant Divinities of the Poets, Bacchus, graceful with thy horns, and you, ye nine Goddesses!

Who can doubt that I should wish the fair one to know how to dance, that, the wine placed on table, she may move her arms in cadence, when requested. Masters of posture, 1072 the representations on the stage, are much valued; so much gracefulness does that pliant art possess. I am ashamed to advise on trifling points, to understand how to throw a cast of dice, and, thy value, the cube when thrown. And now let her throw the three numbers; now let her consider, at which number she can cleverly enter most conveniently, and which one she must call for. 1073 And, with her skill, let her play not amiss at the hostilities of the pieces; 1074 when the single man perishes between his two enemies. How the warrior, too, 1075 wages the war when caught without his companion; and how the enemy full oft retreats on the path on which he has begun. Let the smooth balls, 1076 too, be poured into the open net; and not a ball must be moved but the one which you shall be lifting up. There is a kind of game, 1077 distributed into as many lines on a small scale, as the fleeting year contains months. A little table receives 1078 three pebbles on each side, on which to bring one's own into a straight line, is to gain the victory.

Devise a thousand amusements. 'Tis shocking for the fair one not to know how to play; many a time, while playing, is love commenced. But the least matter is how to use the throws to advantage; 'tis a task of greater consequence to lay a restraint on one's manners. While we are not thinking, and are revealed by our very intentness, and, through the game, our feelings, laid bare, are exposed; anger arises, a disgraceful failing, and the greed for gain; quarrels, too, and strife, and, then, bitter regrets. Recriminations are uttered; the air resounds with the brawl, and every one for himself invokes the angry Divinities. There is no trusting 1079 the tables, and, amid vows, new tables are called for; full oft, too, have I seen cheeks wet with tears. May Jupiter avert from you indiscretions so unbecoming, you, who have a care to be pleasing to any lover.

To the fair, has nature, in softer mood, assigned these amusements; with materials more abundant do the men disport. They have both the flying ball, 1080 and the javelin, and the hoop, and arms, and the horse trained to go round the ring. No plain of Mars receives you, nor does the spring of the Virgin, 1081 so intensely cold; nor does the Etrurian 1082 river carry you along with its smooth stream. But you are allowed, and it is to your advantage, to go in the shade of Pompey's Portico, at the time when the head is heated by the steeds of the Constellation of the Virgin. 1083 Frequent the Palatium, consecrated to the laurel-bearing Phoebus;'twas he that overwhelmed in the deep the ships of Parsetonium. 1084 The memorials, also, which the Bister and the wife 1085 of our Ruler have erected; his son-in-law 1086 too, his head encircled with naval honors. Frequent the altars of the Memphian heifer, 1087 that smoke with frankincense; frequent the three Theatres, 1088 in conspicuous positions. Let the sand, stained with the warm blood, have you for spectators; the goal, also, to be passed with the glowing wheels. 1089

That which lies hid is unknown; for what is not known there is no desire. All advantage is lost, when a pretty face is without one to see it. Were you to excel even Thamyras 1090 and Amcebeus in your singing, there would be no great regard for your lyre, while unknown. If Apelles of Cos 1091 had never painted Venus, she would have lain concealed beneath the ocean waves. What but fame alone is sought by the hallowed Poets? The sum of all my labours has that crowning object. In former days, Poets were 1092 the care of rulers and of kings; and the choirs of old received great rewards. Hallowed was the dignity, and venerable the name of the Poets; and upon them great riches were often bestowed. Ennius, born in the mountains of Calabria, was deemed worthy, great Scipio, to be placed near to thee. 1093 At the present day, the ivy lies abandoned, without any honor; and the laborious anxiety that toils for the learned Muses, receives the appellation of idleness.

But be it our study to lie on the watch for fame; who would have known of Homer, if the Iliad, a never-dying work, had lain concealed? Who would have known of Danâe, if she had been for ever shut up, and if, till an old woman, she had continued concealed in her tower? The throng, ye beauteous fair, is advantageous to you; turn your wandering steps full oft beyond your thresholds. The she-wolf goes on her way to the many sheep, that she may carry off but one; and the bird of Jove pounces down upon the many birds. Let the handsome woman, too, present herself to be seen by the public; out of so many, perhaps there will be one for her to attract. In all places, let her ever be desirous to please; and, with all attention, let her have a care for her charms. Chance is powerful everywhere; let your hook be always hanging ready. In waters where you least think it, there will be a fish. Many a time do the hounds wander in vain over the woody mountains; and sometimes the stag falls in the toils, with no one to pursue him. What was there for Andromeda, when bound, less to hope for, than that her tears could possibly charm any one? Many a time, at the funeral of a husband, is another husband found. To go with the tresses dishevelled, and not to withhold your lamentations, is becoming.

But avoid those men who make dress and good looks their study; and who arrange their locks, each in its own position. What they say to you, they have repeated to a thousand damsels. Their love is roving, and remains firm in no one spot. What is the woman to do, when the man, himself, is still more effeminate, and himself perchance may have still more male admirers?

You will hardly believe me, but still, do believe me; Troy would have been still remaining, if it had followed the advice of its own Priam. 1094 There are some men who range about, under a fictitious appearance of love, and, by means of such introductions, seek disgraceful lucre. And do not let the locks deceive you, shining much with the liquid nard; 1095 nor yet the narrow belt, 1096 pressed upon the folds of their dress. Nor let the robe of finest texture beguile you; nor yet if there shall be many and many a ring 1097 on their fingers. Perhaps the best dressed of the number of these may be some thief, 1098 and may be attracted by a desire for your clothes. "Give me back my property!" full oft do the plundered fair ones cry; "Give me back my property!" the whole Forum resounding with their cries. Thou, Venus, 1099 unmoved, and you, ye Goddesses, 1101 Hear the Appian way, from your temples blazing with plenteous gold, behold these disputes. There are even certain names notorious by a reputation that admits of no doubt; those females who have been deceived by many, share the criminality of their favorites. Learn, then, from the complaints of others, to have apprehensions for yourselves; and do not let your door be open to the knavish man.

Refrain, Cecropian fair, from believing Theseus, 1102 when he swears; the Gods whom he will make his witnesses, he has made so before. And no trust is there left for thee, Demophoôn, heir to the criminality of Theseus, since Phyllis has been deceived. If they are lavish of their promises, in just as many words do you promise them; if they give, do you, too, give the promised favours. That woman could extinguish the watchful flames of Vesta, and could bear off the sacred things, daughter of Inachus, 1103 from thy temples, and could administer to her husband the aconite, mixed with the pounded hemlock, if on receiving a present she could deny a favour.

My feelings are prompting me to go too close; check the rein, my Muse: and be not hurled headlong by the wheels in their full career. Should lines, written on the tablets made of fir, try the soundings; let a maid suited for the duty take in the billets that are sent. Examine them; and collect from the words themselves, whether he only pretends what you are reading, or whether he entreats anxiously, and with sincerity. And after a short delay, write an answer: delay ever stimulates those in love, if it lasts only for a short time.

But neither do you make yourself too cheap to the youth who entreats, nor yet refuse, with disdainful lips, what he is pressing for. Cause him both to fear and to hope at the same moment; and oft as you refuse him, let hopes more assured, and diminished apprehensions arise.

Write your words, ye fair, in a legible hand, but of common parlance, and such as are usual; the recognized forms of language are most pleasing. —

Ah! how oft has the wavering lover been inflamed by a letter, and how oft has uncouth language proved detrimental to, a graceful form! But since, although you are without the honors of the fillet of chastity, it is still your care to deceive your husbands; 1104 let the skilled hand of a maid, or of a boy, carry the tablets, and don't entrust your pledges to some unknown youth. I myself have seen the fair pale with terror on that account, enduring, in their misery, servitude to all future time. Perfidious, indeed, is he who retains such pledges: but still in them he has power equal to the lightnings of Ætna.

In my opinion deceit is allowable, for the purpose of repelling deceit; and the laws permit us to take up arms against the armed. One hand should be accustomed to write in numerous styles. Perdition to those, through whom this advice must be given by me! Nor is it safe to write, except when the wax is quite smoothed over; so that the same tablet may not contain two hands. 1105 Let your lover be always styled a female when you write; in your billets let that be "she," which really is "he."

But I wish to turn my attention from trifles to things of more consequence, and with swelling canvass to expand my filling sails. It conduces to good looks to restrain habits of anger. Fair peace becomes human beings, savage fury wild beasts. With fury the features swell; with blood the veins grow black; the eyes flash more wildly than the Gorgonian fires. "Pipe, hence avaunt, 1106 thou art not of so much worth to me," said Pallas, when she saw her features in the stream. You, too, if you were to look at your mirror in the midst of your anger, hardly could any one distinctly recognize her own countenance. And, in no less degree, let not a repulsive haughtiness sit upon your features; by alluring eyes love must be enticed. Believe me, ye fair who know it by experience, I hate immoderate conceit. Full oft do the features in silence contain the germs of hatred. Look at him who looks on you; smile sweetly in return to him who smiles. Does he nod at you; do you, too, return the sign well understood. When the Boy Cupid has made these preludes, laying aside his foils, he takes his sharp arrows from his quiver.

I hate the melancholy damsels too. Let Ajax be charmed with Tecmessa; 1107 us, a joyous throng, the cheerful woman captivates. Never should I have asked thee, Andromache, nor thee, Tecmessa, that one of you would be my mistress. I seem hardly ably to believe it, though by your fruitfulness I am obliged to believe it, that you could have granted your favours to your husbands. And could, forsooth, that most melancholy woman say to Ajax, "My life!" and words which are wont to please the men?

What forbids me to apply illustrations from great matters to small ones, and not to be standing in awe of the name of a general? To this person the skilful general has entrusted a hundred to be ruled with the twig of vine; 1108 to this one so many cavalry; to that one he has given the standard to defend. Do you, too, consider, to what use each of us is suited, and class each one in his assigned position. Let the rich man give his presents; let him that professes the law, defend; the eloquent man may often plead the cause of his client. We who compose verse, verses alone let us contribute. This throng, before all others, is susceptible of love. Far and wide do we herald the praises of the beauty that pleases us. Nemesis 1109 has fame; Cynthia, too, has fame. The West and the lands of the East know of Lycoris: and many a one is enquiring who my Corinna is. Besides, all deceit is wanting in the hallowed. Poets, and even our art contributes to forming our manners. No ambition influences us, no love of gain; despising the Courts, the couch and the shade are the objects of our commendation. But we are easily attracted, and are consumed by a lasting heat; and we know how to love with a constancy most enduring. Indeed, we have our feelngs softened by the gentle art; and our manners are in conformity with our pursuits.

Be kind, ye fair, to the Aonian bards. In them there is inspiration, and the Pierian maids show favour unto them. In us a Divinity exists: and we have intercourse with the heavens. From the realms of the skies does that inspiration proceed. 'Tis a crime to look for a present from the learned Poets. Ah wretched me! of this crime no fair one stands in dread. Still, do act the dissemblers, and at the very first sight, do not be ravenous. On seeing your nets, a new lover will stop short. But neither can the rider manage with the same reins the horse which has but lately felt the bridle, and that which is well-trained; nor yet must the same path be trod by you in order to captivate the feelings that are steadied by years, and inexperienced youth.

The latter is raw, and now for the first time known in the camp of Love, who, a tender prey, has reached your chamber; with you alone is he acquainted; to you alone would he ever prove constant. Shun a rival; so long as you alone shall possess him, you will be the conqueror. Both sovereignties and love do not last long with one to share in them. The other, the veteran soldier, will love you gradually, and with moderation; and he will put up with much that will not be endured by the novice. He will neither break down your door-posts, nor burn them with raging flames; nor will he fly at the tender cheek of his mistress with his nails. He will neither tear his own clothes, nor yet the clothes of the fair; nor will her torn locks be a cause for grieving. These things befit boys, who are heated with youthful years and with passion: the other, with tranquil feelings, will put up with cruel wounds. With slowly consuming fires will he smoulder, just like a damp torch; or like the wood that has been cut down upon the mountain ridge.

This passion is more sure; the former is short-lived and more bounteous. With speedy hand do you pluck the fruit that passes away.

Let all points be surrendered; the gates we have opened to the enemy, and let confidence be placed in this perfidious betrayal. That which is easily conceded, but badly supports a lasting passion. A repulse must now and then be mingled with your joyous dalliance. Let him lie down before your doors: "Cruel door!" let him exclaim; and let him do many a thing in humble, many in threatening mood. The sweet we cannot endure; with bitter potions we may be refreshed. Full oft does the bark perish, overwhelmed by favouring gales. This it is that does not permit wives to be loved; husbands have access to them, whenever they please. Shut your door, 1110 and let your porter say to you with surly lips, "You cannot come in, desire will seize you as well, thus shut out."

Now lay aside the blunted swords; let the battle be fought with sharpened ones. And I doubt not but that I myself shall be aimed at with weapons of my own furnishing. While the lover that has been captured only of late is falling into your toils, let him hope that he alone has admission to your chamber. But soon let him be aware of a rival, and a division of the privileges of your favours. Remove these contrivances; and his passion will grow effete. Then does the high-mettled courser run well, the starting-place being opened, when he has both competitors to pass by, and those for him to follow. Harshness rekindles the flame, even if gone out. Myself to wit, I confess it, I do not love unless I am ill-used.

Still, the cause for grief should not be too manifest: and in his anxiety he ought to suspect that there is more than what he actually knows. The harsh supervision, too, of some feigned servant should excite him, and the irksome watchfulness of a husband too severe. The pleasure that is enjoyed in safety, is the least valued of all. Though you are more at liberty than even Thais, 1111 still feign apprehensions. Whereas you could do it far better by the door, admit him through the window; and on your countenance show the signs of fear. Let the cunning maid rush in, and exclaim, "We are undone!" and then do you hide the youth in his fright in any spot. Still, an enjoyment without anxiety must be interspersed with his alarms; lest he should not think your favours to be worth so much trouble.

But I was about to omit by what methods the cunning husband may be eluded, and how the watchful keeper. Let the wife stand in awe of her husband; let the safe keeping of a wife be allowed. That is proper; that the laws, and justice, and decency ordain. But for you as well to be watched, whom the Lictor's rod 1112 has but just set at liberty, who can endure it? Come to my sacred rites, that you may learn how to deceive. Even if as many eyes shall be watching you, as Argus had, if there is only a fixed determination, you will deceive them all. And shall a keeper, forsooth, hinder you from being able to write, when an opportunity is given you for taking the bath? When a female confidant can carry the note you have penned, which her broad girth 1113 can conceal in her warm bosom? When she can conceal the paper fastened to her calf, and carry the tender note beneath her sandalled foot.

Should the keeper be proof against these *contrivances*; in place of paper, let your confidant afford her shoulders; and upon her own person let her carry your words. Letters, too, written in new milk, are safe and escape the eye; touch them with powdered coals, and you will read them. The writing, too, which is made with the stalk of wetted flax, 1114 will deceive, and the clean surface will bear the secret marks. The care of watching a fair one fell to Acrisius; still, through his own fault, did she make him a grandsire. What can a keeper do, when there are so many Theatres in the City? When, eagerly she is a spectator of the harnessed steeds? When she is sitting in attendance upon the sistra of the Pharian heifer, and at the place where her male friends are forbidden to go? While, too, the Good Goddess 1115 expels the gaze of males from her temples, except any that, perchance, she bids to come: while, as the keeper watches outside the clothes of the fair, the baths may in safety conceal the lovers who are hiding there; while, so often as is requisite, some pretended she-friend may be sick, and, ill as she is, may give place for her in her couch. While the false key, too, tells 1116 by its name what we are to do, and it is not the door alone that gives the access you require.

The watchfulness of the keeper is eluded by plenty of wine; even though 1117 the grapes be gathered on the hills of Spain. There are drugs, too, which create deep sleep; and let them close the eyes overpowered by Lethæan night. And not amiss does the confidant occupy the troublesome fellow with dalliance to create delay, and in his company spins out the time.

What need is there to be teaching stratagems and trifling precepts, when the keeper may be purchased by the smallest present? Believe me, presents influence both men and Gods: on gifts being presented, Jupiter himself is appeased. What is the wise man to do, when even the fool is gratified with a present? The husband himself, on receiving a present, will be silent. But once only throughout the long year must the keeper be bought; full oft will he hold out the hand which he has once extended.

I complained, I recollect, that new-made friends are to be dreaded; that complaint does not extend to men alone. If you are too trusting, other women will interrupt your pleasures; and this hare of yours will be destined to be hunted down by other persons. Even she, 1118 who so obligingly lends her couch and her room, believe me, has not once only been in my company. And do not let too pretty a maid wait upon you; many a time has she filled 1119 her mistress's place for me. Whither, in my folly, am I led on? Why with bared breast do I strive against the foe, and why, myself, am I betrayed through information that is my own? The bird does not instruct the fowler in which direction he may be taken: the hind does not teach the hostile hounds how to run. Still, let interest see to itself; my precepts, with fidelity will I give. To the Lemnian dames, 1120 for my own destruction, will I present the sword.

Give reason (and 'tis easy to do so) for us to believe ourselves to be loved. Belief arises readily in those who are anxious for the fulfilment of their desires. Let the fair one eye the youth in a kindly manner; let her heave sighs from her very heart, and let her enquire, why it is he comes so late? Let tears be added, too, and feigned apprehensions about a rival, and with her fingers let her tear her face. Soon will he be thoroughly persuaded, one? he will pity you of his own accord; and will say to himself "This woman is consumed by affection for me." Especially, if he shall be well drest, and shall please himself at the looking-glass, he will believe that the Goddesses might be touched with love for him. But, whoever you are, let an injury disturb you only in a moderate degree; and don't, on hearing of a rival, go out of your mind. And don't at once believe it; how injurious it is at once to believe things, Procris will be no slight proof to you.

There is near the empurpled hills of blooming Hymettus a sacred spring, and the ground is soft with the verdant turf. The wood, of no great height, there forms a grove; the strawberry tree overshadows the grass; rosemary, and laurels, and swarthy myrtles give their perfume. Neither the box-trees with their thick foliage and the slender tamarisks, nor yet the tiny trefoil and the garden pine, are wanting there. Moved by the gentle Zephyrs and the balmy air, the leaves of these many kinds, and the tops of the grass quiver. Pleasant was this retreat to Cephalus; 1121 his servants and his hounds left behind, the youth, when weary, often sat down in this spot. And here he was in the habit of repeating, "Come, gentle Aura [breeze], to be received in my bosom, that thou mayst moderate my heat."

Some person, maliciously officious, with retentive lips carried the words he had heard to the timid ears of his wife. Procris, when she heard the name of Aura [breeze], as though of a rival, fainted away, and with this sudden apprehension she was mute. She turned pale, just as the late leaves become wan, which the coming winter has nipped, the clusters now gathered from the vine; and as the quinces 1122 which in their ripeness are bending their boughs; and as the cornels not yet quite fit for food for man. When her senses had returned, she tore her thin garments from off her body with her nails, and wounded her guiltless cheeks. And no delay was there; raving, with dishevelled locks, she flew amid the tracks, like a Bacchanal aroused by the thyrsus. When she had come near the spot, she left her attendants in the valley; and with silent footsteps, in her boldness, she herself stealthily entered the grove. What, Procris, were thy feelings, when thus, in thy frenzy, thou didst he concealed? What the impulse of thy disquieted breast? Each moment, forsooth, wast thou expecting that she would come, whoever Aura might be, and that their criminality would be witnessed with thine eyes.

Now dost thou repent of having come, for indeed thou wouldst not wish to detect him; and now thou art glad; fluctuating affection is tormenting thy breast. There is the spot, and the name, and the informant to bid thee give credence; and the fact that the lover always apprehends that to exist which he dreads. When she beheld the grass beaten down, the impress of his body, her trembling bosom was throbbing with her palpitating heart. And now midday had made the unsubstantial shadows small, and at an equal distance were the evening and the morn. Behold! Cephalus, the offspring of the Cyilenian God, 1123 returns from the woods, and sprinkles his glowing face with water of the fountain. In thy anxiety, Procris, art thou lying concealed. Along the grass he lies as wont, and says, "Ye gentle Zephyrs, and thou Aura [breeze], come hither." When the welcome mistake of the name was thus revealed to the sorrowing fair, both her senses and the real colour of her face returned.

She arose; and the wife, about to rush into the embrace of her husband, by the moving of her body, shook the leaves that were in her way. He, thinking that a wild beast had made the noise, with alacrity snatched up his bow; his arrows were in his right hand. What, wretched man, art thou about? 'Tis no wild beast; keep still thy weapons. Ah wretched me! by thy dart has the fair been pierced. "Ah me!" she cries aloud, "a loving heart hast thou pierced. That spot has ever retained the wound inflicted by Cephalus. Before my time I die, but injured by no rival; this, O Earth, will make thee light when I am entombed. Now is my breath departing in the breeze that I had thus suspected; I sink, alas! close my eyes with those dear hands."

In his sorrowing bosom he supports the dying body of his spouse, and with his tears he bathes her cruel wounds. Her breath departs; and gradually fleeting from her senseless breast, her breath 1124 is received into the mouth of her wretched husband.

But let us return to our path; I must deal with my subject undisguised, that my wearied bark may reach its port. You may be waiting, in fact, for me to escort you to the banquet, and may be requesting my advice in this respect as well. Come late, and enter when the lights are brought in; delay is a friend to passion; a very great stimulant is delay. Even should you be ugly, to the tipsy you will appear charming: and night itself will afford a concealment for your imperfections. Take up your food with your fingers; 1125 the method of eating is something; and do not besmear all your face with your dirty hand. And do not first 1126 take food at home; but cease to eat a little sooner than you could wish, and could have eaten. Had the son of Priam seen Helen greedily devouring, he would have detested her; and he would have said, "That prize of mine is an oaf."

It is more proper and is more becoming for the fair to drink to excess. Thou dost not, Bacchus, consort amiss with the son of Venus. This too, only so far as the head will bear it, and the senses and the feet will be able to perform their duty; 1127 and do not see each object that is single, as double. A woman sprawling along, and drenched in plenteous wine, is a disgusting object; she is worthy to endure the embraces of any kind of fellows. And it is no safe thing when the tables are removed to fall asleep; in sleep many a shocking thing is wont to happen. I feel ashamed to instruct you any further, but genial Dione says, "That which shames you is especially my own province." Let each particular then be known unto you:

> — —modos a corpore certos
>
> Sumite; non omnes una figura decet.
>
> Quse facie prsesignis eris, resupina jaceto:
>
> Spectentur tergo, quîs sua terga placent.
>
> Milanion humeris Atalantes crura ferebat:
>
> Si bona sunt, hoc sunt accipienda modo.
>
> Parva vehatur equo: quod erat longissima, nunquarc
>
> Thebais Hectoreo nupta resedit equo.
>
> Strata premat genibus, paulum cervice reflexâ,
>
> Foemina, per longum conspicienda latus.
>
> Cui femur est juvenile, carent cui pectora mendâ,
>
> Stet vir, in obliquo fusa sit ipsa toro.
>
> Nec tibi turpe puta crinem, ut Phylleia mater,
>
> Solvere: et effusis colla reflecte comis.
>
> Tu quoque, cui rugis uterum Lucina notavit,
>
> Ut celer aversis utere Parthus equis.
>
> Mille modi Veneris. Simplex minimique laboris,
>
> Cum jacet in dextrum semisupina latus,
>
> Sed neque Phoebei tripodes, nec comiger Ammon,
>
> Vera raagis vobis, quam mea Musa, canent.
>
> Si qua fides arti, "quam longo fecimus usu,
>
> Crédité: præstabunt carmiua nostra fidem.

Sentiat ex imis Yenerem resoluta medullis

Foemina: et ex æquo res juvet ilia duos.

Nec blandæ voces, jucundaque murmura cessent;

Nec taceant medus improba verba jocis.

Tu quoque, cui Yeneris sensum natura negavit,

Dulcia mendaci gaudia finge sono.

Infelix, cui torpet hebes locus ille, puella es;

Quo pariter debent foemina virque frui.

Tantum, cum linges, ne sis manifesta caveto:

Effice per motum luminaque ipsa fidem.

Quod juvet: et voces et anhelitus arguat oris.

Ah pudet! arcanas pars habet ista notas.

Gaudia post Yeneris quæ poscet munus amantem,

Ipsa suas nolet pondus habere preces.

And admit not the light in your chamber with the windows wide open; many blemishes of your person more becomingly lie concealed.

My pastime draws to a close; 'tis time to descend from the swans, 1128 that have borne my yoke upon their necks. As once the youths did, so now the fair, as my audience, may inscribe, "Naso was our preceptor," upon their spoils.

FOOTNOTES BOOK- ONE

(701) [For stripes.—Ver. 16. Statius, in the Thebaid, mentions the strictness of the discipline of Chiron. See the Amores, i. El. xiii. 1. 18.]

(702) [Be ye afar.—Ver. 31. He quotes this and the following line in the Tristia, Book ii. 1. 248, to show that it was not his intention, by his precepts, to inculcate breaches of chastity among the Roman matrons. See the Note to the passage, and to the Fasti, Book ii. 1. 30. The 'vitta,' or 'fillet,' was worn solely by women of pure character.]

(703) [The tawny Indians.—Ver. 53. Herodotus considers the Æthiopians to be Indians. According to some, the father of Andromeda was king of Ethiopia; but she is more frequently represented as a native of Joppa, on the coast of Syria.]

(704) [As many stars as.—Ver. 59. Heinsius considers this and the next line to be spurious.]

(705) [Wish a riper fair.—Ver. 63. 'Juvenis,' applied to a female, would mean something more than a mere girl. 'Juventus' was that age in which a person was in his best years, from about twenty to forty.]

(706) [Pompey's Portico.—Ver. 67. He alludes to the Portico which had been erected by Pompey at Rome, and was shaded by plane trees and refreshed by fountains. The Porticos were walks covered with roofs, supported by columns. They were sometimes attached to other buildings, and sometimes were independent of any other edifice. They were much resorted to by those who wished to take exercise without exposure to the heat of the sun. The Porticos of the temples were originally intended for the resort of persons who took part in the rites performed there. Lawsuits were sometimes conducted in the Porticos of Rome, and goods were sold there.]

(707) [The lion of Hercules.il—Ver. 68. The Nemean lion; which formed the Constellation Leo in the Zodiac.]

(708) [Where the mother.—Ver. 69. He alludes to the Theatre and Portico which Augustus built; the former of which received the name of his nephew Marcellus, the latter of his sister Octavia, the mother of Marcellus. After the death of Marcellus, Octavia added a public library to this Portico

at her own expense. Here there were valuable paintings of Minerva, Philip and Alexander, and Hercules on Mount Aeta. Some suppose that the temple of Concord, built by Livia, and mentioned in the Fasti, is here referred to.]

(709) [The Portico of Livia.—Ver. 72. The Portico of Livia was near the street called Suburra. This Portico is also mentioned in the Fasti. We learn from Strabo that it was near the Via Sacra, or Sacred Street.]

(710) [Granddaughters of Belus.—Ver. 73. This was the Portico of the Danaides, in the temple of Apollo. It is referred to in the Second Elegy of the Second Book of the Amores.]

(711) [Bewailed by Venus.—Ver. 75. He alludes to the temple of Venus, at Rome, which, according to Juvenal, was notorious as the scene of intrigues and disgraceful irregularities. It was a custom of the Romans, borrowed from the Assyrians, to lament Adonis in the temple of Venus. See the Tenth Book of the Metamorphoses. This worship of the Assyrians is mentioned by the Prophet Ezekiel, chap. viii. ver. 13, 'women weeping for Thatnmuz.']

(712) [The Jew of Syria.—Ver. 76. He alludes to the rites performed in the Synagogues of the Jews of Rome, on the Sabbath, to which numbers or females were attracted, probably by the music. There were great numbers of Jews at Rome in the reign of Augustus, who were allowed to follow their own worship, according to the law of Moses. The Roman females visiting the Synagogues, assignations and gross irregularities became the consequence. Tiberius withdrew this privilege from the Jews, and ordered the priests' vestments and ornaments to be burnt. This line is thus rendered in Dryden's version:

'Nor shun the Jewish walk, where the foul drove,

On Sabbaths rest from everything but love.'

This wretched paraphrase is excused by the following very illiberal note,

'If this version seems to bear a little hard on the ancient Jews, it does not at all wrong the modern.']

(713) [Many a woman.—Ver. 78. Io, or Isis, was debauched by Jupiter. Martial and Juvenal speak of the irregularities practised on these occasions.]

(714) [Where the erection.—Ver. 81. He refers to the Forum of Cæsar and the temple of Venus, which was built by Julius Cæsar after the battle of Pharsalia.]

(715) [Of Appius.—Ver. 82. He alludes to the aqueduct which had been constructed by the Censor Appius. This passed into the City, through the

Latin gate, and discharged itself near the spot where the temple of Venus was built.]

(716) [Shooting stream. — Ver. 82; He alludes to the violence with which the water was discharged by the pipes of the aqueduct into the reservoir.]

(717) [Which is adjoining. — Ver. 87. The temple of Venus was near the Forum.]

(718) [Ravished Sabine fair. — Ver. 102. See the Fasti, Book iii. 1. 199.]

(719) [Neither did curtains. — Ver. 103. The 'vela,' here referred to, may mean either the 'siparia,' or curtains of the theatres, or the awnings which were hung over them. See the Note on the 'siparia' of the theatres, referred to in the Third Book of the Metamorphoses, L 111. The 'velaria,' or 'awnings,' were stretched over the whole space of the theatres, to protect the spectators from the sun and rain.]

(720) [Marble theatre. — Ver. 103. The Theatres of Pompey and Scaurus were of marble.]

(721) [Nor was the stage. — Ver. 104. The 'pulpita' was that part of the stage where the actors stood who spoke. It was elevated above the orchestra, where the Chorus, and dancers and musicians were placed.]

(722) [Upon the maidens. — Ver. 116. Some writers say that only thirty women were carried off. Valerius Antius made the number 427, and Plutarch mentions a statement that it was 600]

(723) [The partition. — Ver. 141. See the Amores, Book iii. El. ii. 1. 19.]

(724) [Let the usual subjects. — Ver. 144. 'Publica verba' means the compliments of the day,' and the 'topics suited to the occasion.']

(725) [Statues of ivory. — Ver. 149. For an account of this procession, see the Amores, Book iii. El. ii. 1. 43.]

(726) [Your fingers. — Ver. 150. See 1. 42, of the same Elegy.]

(727) [Dirty ground. — Ver. 154. See 1. 26, of the same Elegy.]

(728) [Knee against it. — Ver. 158. See 1. 24, of the same Elegy.]

(729) [With his ready hand. — Ver. 160. As the seats of the Circus were hard, the women often made use of a cushion to sit upon. Those who were not so fortunate as to get a front seat, and so rest their feet in the railings opposite (see the Second Elegy of the Third Book of the Amores, 1. 64, and the Note), used a footstool, 'scamnum,' (which is mentioned here in the 162nd line,) on which they rested their feet.]

(730) [Its sad duties.—Ver. 164. Juvenal tells us that gladiatorial spectacles were sometimes exhibited in the Forum.]

(731) [Himself receives a wound.—Ver. 166. The word 'habet,' here used, is borrowed from the usage at the gladiatorial games. When a gladiator was wounded, the people called aloud 'habet,' or 'hoc habet and the one who was vanquished lowered his arms, in token of submission. If the people chose that he should be saved, they pressed down their thumbs; but they turned them up, if they desired that he should be killed.]

(732) [Asking for the racing list.—Ver. 167. The 'libellus,' here mentioned, was the list of the horses, with their names and colours, and those of the drivers. It served the same purpose as the race-cards on our courses.]

(733) [Having deposited the stake.—Ver. 168. When a bet was made, the parties betting gave to each other a pledge, 'pignus,' in the shape of some trinket, such as a ring. When the bet was completed, they touched hands.]

(734) [When of late.—Ver. 171. He speaks of a 'Naumachia,' or mimic sea-fight, which had been lately exhibited at Rome by Augustus, in commemoration of the battle of Actium. As Antony had collected his forces from the East and all parts of Greece, his ships are alluded to as the Persian and Cecropian, or Athenian ships. The term, 'Naumachia,' was applied both to the representation of a sea-fight, and to the place where it was given. They were sometimes exhibited in the Circus or Amphitheatre, the water being introduced under-ground, but more generally in spots constructed for the purpose. The first was shown by Julius Cæsar, who caused a lake to be dug for the purpose in a part of the Campus Martius, which Suetonius calls 'the lesser Codeta.' This was filled up by Augustus, who dug a lake near the Tiber for the same purpose; to which, probably, reference is here made.]

(735) [Introduced.—Ver. 172. 'Induxit.' By the use of this word, it would seem that Augustus Cæsar introduced the ships, probably, from the river Tiber into the lake.]

(736) [See! Cæsar prepares.—Ver. 177. Augustus sent his grandson, Caius, the son of his daughter Julia and Agrippa, to head an expedition against Phraates, the king of the Parthians, the conquerors of Crassus; from this expedition he did not live to return, but perished in battle.]

(737) [Crassi, rejoice.—Ver. 180. See the Fasti, Book v. 1. 583-8, with the Note. Also Book vi. 1. 465]

(738) [Of the Gods.—Ver. 183. In a spirit of adulation, he deifies Caius Cæsar, and his brother Lucius.]

(739) [First of the youths.—Ver. 194. The 'princeps juvenum' had the honour of riding first, in the review of the Equestrian ranks by the Emperor. See the Tristia, Book ii. 1. 90. Caius did not live to fulfil this prophecy, as he was slain through the perfidy of the Parthian general.]

(740) [Since thou hast brothers.—Ver. 195. He alludes, probably, to Lucius Cæsar, the other grandson of Augustus, and Marcus Agrippa, the husband of Julia, the daughter of Augustus.]

(741) [Hast a sire.—Ver. 196. He had been adopted by Augustus. *What rivers are borne.—Ver. 220. See the twentieth line of the Second Elegy, Book iv. of the Tristia. * Perfectly well.—Ver. 222. See a similar passage in the Tristia' Book iv. EL ii. 1. 24.]

(742) [The Euphrates.—Ver. 223. The rivers were generally personified by the ancients as being crowned with reeds.]

(743) [The one whose.—Ver. 224. The young man is supposed to be addressing the damsel in these words.]

(744) [From Danaë.—Ver. 225. He means, that Persia was so called from Perses, the son of Andromeda, by Perseus, the son of Danaë. It is more generally thought to have been so called from a word signifying; a horse.' Achæmenes was one of the ancient kings of Persia.]

(745) [Still it is fatal.—Ver. 236. 'Solet,' 'is wont,' is certainly a pre-narrative reading here to 'nocet.']

(746) [Deceiving lamp.—Ver. 245. This is as much as to remind him of the adage that women and linen look best by candle-light.]

(747) [Why mention Baiæ.—Ver. 255. Baiæ was a town on the sea-shore, near Naples, famous for its hot baths. It was delightfully situate, and here Pompey, Caesar, and many of the wealthy Romans, had country seats: Seneca and Propertius refer to it as famous for its debaucheries, and it was much frequented by persons of loose character. It was the custom at Baiæ, in the summer-time, for both sexes to cruise about the shore in boats of various colours, both in the day-time and at night, with sumptuous feasts and bands of music on board.]

(748) [Hostile hand.—Ver. 260. See the Fasti, Book iii. 1. 263. He means that the Arician grove was much resorted to by those engaged in courtship tad intrigues.]

(749) [Borne upon unequal wheels.—Ver. 264. He alludes to Thalia, the Muse who inspires him, preferring the unequal or Hexameter and Pentameter measure of Elegiac verse.]

(750) [By the lark.—Ver. 286. See the Metamorphoses, Book x.]

(751) [Of Cydon.'—Ver. 293. This was a city of Crete.]

(752) [Untruthful as it is.—Ver. 298. The Cretans were universally noted in ancient times for their disregard for truth. St. Paul, in his Epistle to Titus, ch. i. ver, 12, says, quoting from the Cretan poet Epimenides "One of themselves, even a prophet of their own, said, 'The Cretans are alway liars, evil beasts, slow bellies.' This witness is true."]

(753) [By a bull!—Ver. 302. See this story explained in the Translation of the Metamorphoses.]

(754) [The sire.—Ver. 326. This was the Minotaur. See the Metamorphoses, Book viii]

(755) [If the Cretan dame.—Ver. 327. This was Ærope, the wife of Atreus, who slew the children of his brother Thyestes, and set them on table before their father.]

(756) [Who spoiled.—-Ver. 331. He falls into his usual mistake of confounding Scylla, the daughter of Nisus, with the daughter of Phorcys.]

(757) [The flames.—Ver. 335. See the Metamorphoses, Book vii. 1. 391, and the Epistle of Medea to Jason.]

(758) [The son of Amyntor.—Ver. 337. Phoenix, the son of Amyntor, according to Homer, became blind in his latter years. See the Note to the 307th line of the Eighth Book of the Metamorphoses.]

(759) [Of thy guiltless sons.—Ver. 339. Phineus was a king of Arcadia, or, according to some, of Thrace or Paphlagonia. His wife, Cleopatra, being dead or divorced, he married a Scythian, named Harpalice, at whose suggestion he put out the eyes of his sons by Cleopatra. He was persecuted by the Harpies, as a punishment.]

(760) [What is one's own.—Ver. 348. 'Suis' seems preferable here to suos.']

(761) [The crop.—Ver. 349. These lines are referred to by Juvenal in the Fourteenth Satire, 1.143.]

(762) [Your access easy.—Ver. 352. See his address to Nape, in the Amores, Book i. El. ii. Cypassis seems to have been a choice specimen of this class. See the Amores, Book ii. El. viii.]

(763) [Pay him in return.'—Ver. 370. This seems to mean, 'I do not think you can make sufficient return for his ardent affection,' referring to the lover. Some of the Commentators think that it signifies a hint from the servant, that as her mistress's husband has offended her by his infidelities, she ought to repay him in his own coin.]

(764) [Is of use.—Ver. 375. This abominable notion seems to have been acted upon by the Poet himself. See the Amores, Book ii. El. viii.]

(765) [Her birthday.—Ver. 405. See the Amores, Book i. El. viii. 1. 94.]

(766) [Whether the Calends.—Ver. 405. The Matronalia were celebrated on the first day of the Calends of March. It was usual on that day, for husbands to make presents to their wives, and lovers to the objects of their affection. The Calends of March preceded April, which month was sacred to Venus. See the Fasti, Book iii. 1. 170.]

(767) [The wealth of kings.—Ver. 408. It was the custom to bring the spoils of the enemy, or the most curious portions of it, to Rome, where it was exposed to view in the Circus and the Theatres. Ovid tells his readers that they must not think that the ladies can give them any of their leisure on such occasions, as, being so much engaged with the sights, they will have no time for love-making.]

(768) [Pleiades prevail.—Ver. 409. This is said figuratively.]

(769) [Tearful Allia.—Ver. 413. The 16th of July, the day on which the Romans were defeated by the Gauls at the Allia, was deemed unlucky, and no business was transacted on it.]

(770) [A day not suited for.—Ver. 415. The Jews are here alluded to. and he refers to their Sabbath. How some Commentators can have dreamed that the feast of the Saturnalia is referred to, it is hard to say.]

(771) [Great must be.—Ver. 417. The meaning is, 'Be careful not to make your first advances on the birthday of your mistress, as that is the time for making presents, and you will certainly be out of pocket.' See the Amores, Book i. El. viii. 1. 94, and the Note.]

(772) [The loosely-clad pedlar.—Ver. 421. Institor' was properly a person who sold wares, and kept a 'taberna' or 'shop' on account of another. Sometimes free persons, but more frequently slaves, were 'institores.']

(773) [A promissory note.—Ver. 428. 'Syngraphus/ or 'syngrapha,' was a 'bill' 'bond,' or 'promissory note,' which was most probably the kind of writing that the pedlar would here require. It may possibly mean a cheque upon his bankers, the 'argentarii' of Rome.]

(774) [Not to have learned.—Ver. 428. The reading here seems to be non didicisse juvat.' 4 It is not to your advantage that you have learned (to write).' The other reading, 'ne didicisse juvet,' may be rendered, '(perhaps) it may be no advantage that you have learned (to write).']

(775) [Birth day cake.—Ver. 429. See the Amores, Book i. El. viii. 1. 94.]

(776) [The jewel.—Ver. 432. For an account of the earrings of the ancients, see the Notes to the Metamorphoses, Book x. 1. 116.]

(777) [Should you give her.—Ver. 447. The meaning of this and the following line is very obscure; so much so that Burmann is in doubt on the subject. It, however, seems to be, that it is not discreet, on first acquaintance, to give presents, as the damsel may then have a reason for peremptoily giving you up; she carries off your gift, and gives no favour in return.]

(778) [Upon an apple.—Ver. 457: See the twentieth and twenty-first Epistles in the present volume.]

(779) [Extend their hands.—Ver. 462. This figure is taken from the gladiatorial games, where the conquered extended their hands in token of submission.]

(780) [Ring of iron.—Ver. 473. The rings worn by the lower classes were of iron.]

(781) [Under some of the columns.1—Ver. 490. The learned Heinsius absolutely thinks that 'columnas' here means 'mile-stones'! It is pretty clear that Ovid alludes to the columns of the Portico; and he seems to say, that the attentive lover, when he sees the damsel at some distance before him, is not to hesitate to escape the crowd by going into the open space outside of the columns, and then running on, for the purpose of overtaking her. See the Tristia, Book iii. El. iii, where he makes mention of the columns in the Portico of the Danaides.]

(782) [Actor is dancing.—Ver. 501. See the Tristia, Book ii. i. 497.]

(783) [With the irons.'—Ver. 505. See the Amores, Book i. El. xiv 1 25, and the Note. The effeminate among the Romans were very fond of having their hair in curls.]

(784) [With the rough pumice.—Ver. 506. Pliny the Elder mentions pumice stone as 'a substance used by women in washing their bodies, and now by men as well.' Persius, in his Fourth Satire, inveighs against this effeminate practice.]

(785) [Bid those do this.—Ver. 507'. He alludes to the Galli, the eunuch priests of Cybele.]

(786) [Hippolytus.—Ver. 511. Phædra, in her Epistle, alludes to his neglect of dress, as one of the merits of Hippolytus.]

(787) [Plain of Mars.—Ver. 513. The Roman youth practised wrestling, and other athletic exercises, on the Campus Martius Being often stripped naked, or nearly so, the oil, combined with t he heat, would tend to bronze the skin.]

(788) [Not be clammy.—Ver. 515. Probably this is the meaning of 'lingua ne rigeat,' although Nisard's French translation has it, 'let your tongue have no roughness.' Dryden's translation is, of course, of no assistance, as it carefully avoids all the difficult passages.]

(789) [The father of the flock.—Ver. 522. He alludes to the rank smell to the arm-pits, which the Romans called by the name 'hircus,' 'a goat,' from a supposed similarity to the strong smell of that animal.]

(790) [Awaking from her sleep.—Ver. 529. See the Epistle of Ariadne to Theseus.]

(791) [Mimallonian females.—Ver. 541. It is a matter of doubt why the Bacchanalian women were called Mimallonides. According to some, they are so called from Mimas, a mountain of Asia Minor, where the rites of Bacchus were celebrated. Suidas says that they are so called, from 'imitation,' because they imitated the actions of men. Bochart thinks that the word is of Hebrew origin, and that they receive their name from 'memelleran,' 'garrulous' or 'noisy'; or else from mamal,' a 'wine- press.']

(792) [Drunken old man.—Ver. 543. See the adventure of Silenus, in the beginning of Book xi. of the Metamorphoses; and in the Fasti, Book iii. 1. 742. He seems to have been always getting into trouble.]

(793) [Cretan Diadem.—Ver. 558. See the Fasti. Book iii. 1. 516.]

(794) [Evie, Evoë!—Ver. 563. In the combat with the Giants, Jupiter is said, when one of them was slain by Bacchus, to have exclaimed 'Well done, son:' whence the exclamation 'Evie!' was said to have originated. See the Metamorchoses, Book iv. 1. 11 and 15, and the Note.]

(795) [On the table.'—Ver. 572. See the Epistle of Paris to Helen; and the Amores, Book i. El. iv. 1. 20, and Book ii. El. v. 1. 17, and the Notes.]

(796) [From the side.—Ver. 576. See the Amores, Book i. EL iv. 1. 32.]

(797) [Touched with her fingers.—Ver. 577. The ancients are supposed not to have used at meals any implement such as a knife or fork, but merely to have used the fingers only, except in eating soups or other liquids, or jellies, when they employed spoons, which were denoted by the names 'cochlear' and 'ligula.' At meals the Greeks wiped their fingers on pieces

of bread; the Romans washed them with water, and dried them on napkins handed round by the slaves.]

(798) [Are drinking by lot. — Ver. 581. The 'modimperator,' or 'master of the banquet,' was often chosen by lot by the guests, and it was his province to prescribe how much each person should drink. Lots were also thrown, by means of the dice, to show in what order each person was to drink. This passage will show the falsity of his plea in the Second Book of the Tristia, addressed to Augustus, where he says that it was not his intention to address the married women of Rome, but only those who did not wear the 'vittæ' and the 'instita,' the badges of chastity.]

(799) [Agent attends even too much. — Ver. 587. His meaning seems to be, that in the same way as the agent does more than attend to the injunctions of his principal, and puts himself in a position to profit by his office, so is the inamorato, through the confidence of the husband reposed in him, to make a profit that has never been anticipated.]

(801) [Eurytion. — Ver. 593. At the nuptials of Pirithous and Hippodamia. See the Metamorphoses, Book xii. 1. 220, where he is called Eurytus.]

(802) [Stealing up. — Ver. 605. This piece of impudence he professes to practise in the Amores, Book i. El iv. 1. 56.]

(803) [Bird of Juno. — Ver. 627. This fact, in natural history, was probably known only to Ovid, or the peacocks of the present day may be less vain than the Roman ones. See the Metamorphoses, Book i. 1. 723.]

(804) [That there should be Gods. — Ver. 637. This was the avowed opinion of some of the philosophers and atheists of antiquity. We learn from Tertullian that Diogenes, being asked if the Gods exist, answered that he did not know anything about it, but that they ought to exist. The doctrine of the Epicureans was, that the Gods lived a happy and easy life, were not susceptible of anger, and did not trouble themselves about men.]

(805) [Went to Busiris. — Ver. 649. See the Tristia, Book iii. El. xi. 1. 39, where the story of Phalaris is also referred to. Thrasius was the brother of Pygmalion, and was justly punished by Busiris for his cruel suggestion.]

(806) [Phoebe suffered — Ver. 679. See the story of the rape of Phoebe, by Castor and Pollux, in the Fasti, Book v. 1. 699.]

(807) [Work-baskets. — Ver. 693. See the Note to the seventy-third line of the Ninth Epistle.]

(808) [Heroines of olden times. — Ver. 713. Such as Danaë, Europa Seraele, Alcmena, Io, Calisto, Antiope, Maia, Electra, and others.]

(809) [Chaplet of Pallas.—Ver. 727. A crown of olive was presented to the victors in the athletic exercises at the Olympic games.]

(810) [Love for Lyrice.—Ver. 731. If Lyrice here is a female name, it is not known who she was.]

(811) [Daphnis.—Ver. 732. He was a Sicilian, the son of Mercury; and the inventor of Bucolic poetry.]

(812) [Pylades.—Ver. 745: Hermione was the wife of Orestes, the friend of Pylades.]

(813) [With a dart.—Ver. 763. It appears by this, that it was the custom to take fish by striking them with a javelin Salmon ere foretimes caught in a similar manner at the present day.]

FOOTNOTES BOOK- TWO

(901) [Sing, 'Io Pean.'—Ver. 1. This was the usual cry of the hunters, who thus addressed Apollo, the God of the chase, when the prey had been captured iu the toils. See the Metamorphoses, Book iv. 1. 513.]

(902) [Amyclæ.—Ver. 5. A town of Laconia. See the Metamorphoses, Book x. 1. 219, and the Note.]

(903) [Erato.—Ver. 16. He addresses himself to this Muse, as her name was derived from the Greek 'love.' It has been suggested that he had another reason for addressing her, as she was thought to take pleasure in warfare, a state which sometimes, by way of variety, exists between lovers.]

(904) [A bold path.—Ver. 22. This story is again related in the Eighth Book of the Metamorphoses.]

(905) [Like oars.—Ver. 45. He aptly compares the arrangement of the main feathers of a wing to a row of oars.]

(906) [Orion.'—Ver. 56. So in the Metamorphoses, Book v. 1. 206, he says to his son Icarus, 'Fly between both: and I bid thee neither to look at Bootes, nor Helice, nor the drawn sword of Orion.']

(907) [Is angling.—Ver. 77. There is a similar passage in the Metamorphoses, 1. 216.]

(908) [The Clarian God.—Ver. 80. See the Fasti, Book i. 1. 20, and the Note.]

(909) [And Calymne.—Ver. 81. These peaces are mentioned in the corresponding passages in the Metamorphoses, Book viii. 1. 222.]

(910) [Astypalæa..—Ver. 82. This was an isle in the group of the Sporades, between Crete and the Cyclades. It contained but one city, and was long and narrow, and of rugged appearance.]

(911) [The young horse.—Ver. 100. See the Amoves. Book i. El. viii 1. 8, and the Note.]

(912) [The Marsian spells.—Ver. 102. The 'naenia' was a mournful dirge or chaunt uttered by the sorcerer in his incantations. On the Marsi, see the Sixth Book of the Fasti, 1. 142, and the Note to the passage.]

(913) [Causing paleness.—Ver. 105. Philtres were noxious potions, made of venomous or stimulating ingredients, prescribed as a means of gaining the affections of the person to whom they were administered.]

(914) [Nireus.—Ver. 109. See the Pontic Epistles, Book iv. Ep. xiii. 1. 16, and the Note to the passage.]

(915) [Charming Hylas.—Ver. 110. See the Tristia, Book ii. 1.]

(916) [Ocean Goddesses.—Ver. 124. Calypso was really the only sea Goddess that was enamoured of Ulysses. Circe was not a sea Goddess.]

(917) [Blood of Dolon.'—Ver. 135. See the Metamorphoses, Book xiii. line 244.]

(918) [Hjemontan horses—Ver. 136. The steeds of Achilles.]

(919) [The Chaonian bird.—Ver. 150. Chaonia was a district of Epirus, said to have been so called from Chaon, a Trojan. Dodona was in Epirus, and in its forests were said to be doves that had the gift of prophecy. See the Translation of the Metamorphoses .]

(920) [Resort to law.—Ver. 151. He means to say 'let man and wife be always thinking about resorting to law to procure a divorce.']

(921) [1 gave verses.—Ver. 166. He intends a pun here. 'Verba dare' is 'to deceive,' but literally it means 'to give words.' See the Amores, book i. El. viii. 1. 57.]

(922) [Atalanta of Nonacris.—Ver. 185. See the Amores, Book iii. El. ii. 29, and the Note.]

(923) [Bow of Hylceus.—Ver. 191. Hylæus and Rhæcus were Centaurs, who were pierced by Atalanta with her arrows, for making an attempt on her chastity. He alludes to the bow of Cupid in the next line.]

(924) [The ivory cubes.'—Ver. 203. He alludes to throws of the 'tali' and 'tessera,' which were different kinds of dice. See the Note to 1. Footnote 471: of the Second Book of the Tristia. In this line he seems to mean the 'tessera,' which were similar to our dice, while the 'tali,' which he next mentions, had only four flat surfaces, being made in imitation of the knuckle-bones of animals, and having two sides uneven and rounded. The dice were thrown on a table, made for the purpose, with an elevated rim. Some throws, like our doublets, are supposed to have counted for more than the number turned up. The most fortunate throw was called 'Venus.' or 'Venereus jactus'; it is thought to have consisted of a combination, making fourteen, the dice presenting different numbers. Games with dice were only sanctioned by law as a pastime during meals.]

(925) [Make bad moves.—Ver. 204. 'Dare jacta' means 'to move the throws,' in allusion to the game of 'duodecim scripta,' or 'twelve points,' which was played with counters moved according to the throws of the dice, probably in a manner not unlike our game of backgammon. The hoard was marked with twelve lines, on which the pieces moved.]

(926) [Or if you are throwing.—Ver. 205. By the use of the word 'seu, or,' we must suppose that he has, under the word 'numeri,' alluded to the game with the 'tesseræ,' or six-sided dice.]

(927) [The game that imitates.—Ver. 207. He here alludes to the 'ludus latrunculorum,' literally 'the game of theft,' which is supposed to have been somewhat similar to our chess. He refers to its name in the words, 'latrocinii sub imagine.' The game was supposed to imitate the furtive stratagems of warfare: hence the men, which were usually styled 'calculi,' were also called by the name of 'latrones,' 'latrunculi,' 'milites,' 'bella-tores,' 'thieves,' 'little thieves,' 'soldiers,' 'warriors.' As we see by the next line, they were usually made of glass, though sometimes more costly materials were employed. The skill of this game consisted either in taking the pieces of the adversary, or rendering them unable to move. The first was done when the adversary's piece was brought by the other between two of his own. See the Tristia, Book ii. 1.477. The second took place when the pieces were 'ligati,' or 'ad incitas redacti,' brought upon the last line and unable to move. White and red are supposed to have been the colour of the men. This game was much played by the Roman ladies and nobles.]

(928) [Hold the screen.—Ver. 209. The ancients used 'umbracula,' or screens against the weather (resembling our umbrellas), which the Greeks called — — — —. They were used generally for the same purposes as our parasols, a protection against the heat of the sun. They seem not to have been in general carried by the ladies themselves, but by female slaves, who held them over their mistresses. See the Fasti, Book ii. 1. 209. These screens, or umbrellas, were much used by the Roman ladies in the amphitheatre, to protect them from sun and rain, when the 'velarium,' or awning, was not extended.]

(929) [Tasteful couch.'—Ver. 211. This was probably the 'triclinium' on which they reposed at meals. The shoes were taken off before reclining on it. Female slaves did this office for the ladies, and males for the men.]

(930) [Looking-glass.—Ver. 216. These were generally held by female slaves, when used by their mistresses. See the Metamorphoses, Book iv. 1. 349. and the Note.]

(931) [Held the work-basket.—Ver. 219. Hercules, who Wiled the serpents sent by Juno, is reproached for doing this, by Deianira in her Epistle.]

(932) [As though a servant.—Ver. 228. He is to be ready, if his mistress goes to a party, to act the part of the slave, who was called 'adversitor,' whose duty it was to escort his master home in the evening, if it was dark, with a lighted torch.]

(933) [A vehicle.—Ver. 230. 'Rota,' a wheel, is, by Synecdoche, used to signify 'a vehicle.']

(934) [Cynthius.—Ver. 240. See the Note to line 51, of the Epistle from Aenone to Paris.]

(935) [Through the open roof.—Ver. 245. He gives a somewhat hazardous piece of advice here; as he instructs him to obtain admission by climbing up the wall, and getting in at the skylight, which extended over the 'atrium,' or 'court,' a room which occupied the middle of the house. The Roman houses had, in general, but one story over the ground-floor.]

(936) [The high window.—Ver. 246. This passage may be illustrated by the Note to 1. 752: of Book xiv. of the Metamorphoses.]

(937) [Day on which.—Ver. 257. He alluded to a festival celebrated by the servants, on the Caprotine Nones, the seventh of July, when they sacrificed to 'Juno Caprotina.' Macrobius says that the servants sacrificed to Juno under a wild fig-tree (called 'caprificus'), in memory of the service done by the female slaves, in exposing themselves to the lust ot the enemy, for the public welfare. The Gauls being driven from the city, the neighbouring nations chose the Dictator of the Fidenates for their chief, and, marching to Rome, demanded of the Senate, that if they would save their city, they should send out to them their wives and daughters The Senate, knowing their own weakness, were much perplexed, when a handmaid, named 'Tutela,' or 'Philotis,' offered, with some others, to go out to the enemy in disguise. Being, accordingly, dressed like free women, they repaired in tears to the camp of the enemy. They soon induced their new acquaintances to drink, on the pretence that they were bound to consider the day as a festival; and when intoxicated, a signal was giver, from a fig tree near, that the Romans should fall on them. The camp of the enemy was assailed, and most of them were slain. In return for their service, the female, slaves were made free, and received marriage portion? at the public expense. Another account, agreeing with the present passage, says, that the Gauls were the enemy who made the demand, and that Retana was the name of the female slave.]

(938) [The lower classes.—Ver. 259. Witness his own appeals in the Amores to Napè, Cypassis. Bagous, and the porter.]

(939) [In the Sacred Street.'—Ver. 266. Presents of game and trout very often follow a similar devolution at the present day.]

(940) [Amaryllis was so fond of.—Ver. 267. He alludes to a line of Virgil, which, doubtless, was then well known to all persons of education. It occurs in the Eclogues: 'Castaneasque nuces, mea quas Amaryllis amabat.' 'Chesnuts, too, which my Amaryllis was so fond of.' In the next line, he hints that the damsels of his day were too greedy to be satisfied with chesnuts only.]

(941) [Thrush and a pigeon.—Ver. 269. Probably live birds of the kind are here alluded to; Pliny tells us that they were trained to imitate the human voice. Thrushes were much esteemed as a delicacy for the table. They were sold tied up in clusters, in the shape of a crown.]

(942) [By these means.—Ver. 271. He alludes to those who continued to slip into dead men's shoes, by making trifling presents of niceties. Juvenal inveighs against this practice.]

(943) [Poetry does not.—Ver. 274. See the remarks of Dipsas in the Amores, Book i. El. viii. 1. 57.]

(944) [Only rich.—Ver. 276. See the Amores, Book iii. El. ii.]

(945) [Tyrian hue.—Ver. 297. See the Fasti, Book ii. 1. 107, and the Note.]

(946) [Of Cos—Ver. 298. See the Epistles of Sabinus, Ep. iii. 1. 45, and the Note.]

(947) [A dress of felt.—Ver. 300. 'Gausape,' 'gausapa,' or 'gausapum,' was a kind of thick woolly cloth, which had a long nap on one side. It was used to cover tables and beds, and as a protection against wind and rain. It was worn both by males and females, and came into use among the Romans about the time of Augustus.]

(948) [You are setting me on fire.—Ver. 301. Burmanu deservedly censures the explanation of 'moves incendia,' given by Crispinus, the Delphin Editor, 'Vous mourrez de chaud,' 'You will die of heat,' applying the observation to the lady, and not, figuratively, to the feelings of her lover.]

(949) [Her very embraces.—Ver. 308. The common reading of this line is clearly corrupt; probably the reading is the one here adopted, 'Et un dat, gaudia, voce proba.']

(950) [What advice—Ver. 368. These attempts at argument are exhausted by Paris, in his Epistle to Helen.]

(952) [Stinging-nettle.—Ver. 417. Pliny prescribes nettle-seed as a stimulating medicine, mixed with linseed, hyssop, and pepper.]

(953) [White onion.—Ver. 421. The onions of Megara are praised by Cato, the agricultural writer.]

(954) [Alcathous.—Ver. 421. See the Metamorphoses, Book vii. 1.]

(955) [At first.—Ver. 467. See the beginning of the First Book of the Metamorphoses.]

(956) [Unclean mate.—Ver. 486. He alludes to the strong smell of the he-goat.]

(957) [Machaon.—Ver. 491. He was a famous physician, son of Æsculapius, and was slain in the Trojan war. See the Tristia, Book v. El. vi. 1. 11.]

(958) [He came.—Ver. 496. 'Adest' seems a preferable reading to 'agit.']

(959) [To know himself.—Ver. 600. 'Know thyself,' was a saying of Chilo, the Lacedaemonian, one of the wise men of Greece. This maxim was also inscribed in gold letters in the temple of Apollo at Delphi. 'Too much of nothing' was a second maxim there inscribed; and a third was, 'Misery is the consequence of debt and discord.']

(960) [Drinks with elegance.—Ver. 506. It is hard to say what art in drinking is here alluded to; whether a graceful air in holding the cup, or the ability of drinking much without shewing any signs of inebriety.

Let the old woman come.—Ver. 329. In sickness it was the custom to purify the bed and chamber of the patient, with sulphur and eggs. It seems also to have been done when the patient was pining through unrequited love. Apulius mentions a purification by the priest of Isis, who uses eggs and sulphur while holding a torch and repeating a prayer. The nurse of the patient seems here to be directed to perform the ceremony.]

(961) [The Fasti, Book ii. 1. 19, and Book iv. 1. 728. From a passage of Juvenal, we find that it was a common practice to purify with eggs and sulphur, in the month of September, * On Athos.—Ver. 517. See the Metamorphoses, Book ii. 1. 217, and the Note.]

(962) [On Hybla.—Ver. 517. See the Tristia, Book v. El. xiii. 1. 22.]

(963) [Off your head.—Ver. 528. Iphis, in the fourteenth Book of the Metamorphoses, 1. 732, raises his eyes to the door-posts of his mistress, 'so often adorned by him with wreaths.']

(964) [The senses.—Ver. 532. He seems to believe, with Nixon d'Enelos, in the existence of a sixth sense.]

(965) [Of mighty Jove. — Ver. 540. He alludes to the triumphal procession to the Capitol.]

(966) [Gentle sleep. — Ver. 546. See the Amores, Book iii. El. i. 1. 51. He means to say that husbands give a certain latitude to their wives, who do not fail to improve upon it.]

(967) [Own husband. — Ver. 551. See the Amores, Book i. El. iv. 1. 38.]

(968) [Other men visit. — Ver. 554. 'Viri' seems to be a better reading than 'viro.']

(969) [Mars and Venus. — Ver. 562. See the Metamorphoses, Book iv. 1. 173.]

(970) [Says, laughing. — Ver. 585. See a similar passage in the Metamorphoses, Book iv. 1. 187.]

(971) [For Thrace. — Ver. 588. He was much venerated by the warlike Thracians.]

(972) [Paphos. — Ver. 588. See the Metamorphoses, Book x. 1. 298.]

(973) [Fire and water render. — Ver. 598. Among the Romans, when the bride reached her husband's house, he received her with fire and water, which it was the custom for her to touch. This is, by some, supposed to have been symbolical of purification; or it was an expression of welcome, as the interdiction of fire and water was the formula for banishment.]

(974) [My sallies. — Ver. 600. See Book L 1. 31, and the Note. See also the Fasti, Book iv. 1. 866, and the Note.]

(975) [The rites of Ceres. — Ver. 601. He alludes to the mysterious rites of Ceres, in the island of Samothrace.]

(976) [Not enclosed in chests. — Ver. 609. Certain chests were carried in the procession at the festival of Ceres, the contents of which, if there were any, was a mystery to the uninitiated.]

(977) [The left hand. — Ver. 614. This is the attitude of the Venus de Medicis.]

(978) [At a heavy price. — Ver. 626. Men spend their money on debauchery, only for the pleasure of talking of it.]

(979) [Waving wings. — Ver. 644. He refers to Perseus admiring the swarthy Andromeda.]

(980) [Of larger stature. — Ver. 645. She was remarkable for her height.]

(981) [Green bark. — Ver. 639. He speaks of the slip engrafted in the stock.]

(982) [What Consulship.—Ver. 663. The age of persons was reckoned by naming the Consulship in which they were born; the period of which was Known by reference to the 'Fasti Consulares.' See the Introduction to the Fasti.]

(983) [Rigid Censor.—Ver. 664. It was the duty of the Censor to make enquiries into the age of all individuals.]

(984) [Best years.—Ver. 666. Even in those days, it was considered ungallant to make too scrutinizing enquiries into the years of ladies of 'a certain age.']

(985) [Kind of warfare.—Ver. 674. See the Amores, Book i. El. ix. 1. 1.]

(986) [Besides in these.—Ver. 675. In reference to females of a more advanced age.]

(987) [Seven times five years.—Ver. 694. He probably means, in this passage, a lustrum of five years. Burmann justly observes, that 'cito,' 'quickly,' or 'soon,' can hardly be the proper reading, as it seems to contradict the meaning of the context. He suggests 'nisi,' meaning 'but,' or 'only.' See the Fasti, Book iii. 1. 166, and the Note. Also the Tristia, Book iv. El. xvi. 1. 78.]

(988) [Stored up in the times.—Ver. 696. He uses this metaphorical expression to signify that he admires females when of a ripe and mature age See the Amores, Book ii. El. v. 1. 54, and the Note.]

(989) [The shooting grass.—Ver. 698. In Nisard's translation, the words 'prata novella' are rendered 'l'herbe nouvellement coupée,' 'the grass newly cut.' This is not the meaning of the passage. He intends to say that the grass just shooting up is apt to cut or prick the naked foot.]

(990) [Hermione.—Ver. 699. She was the daughter of Helen and Menelaus.]

(991) [Gorge.—Ver. 700. She was the daughter of Altnea, and sister of Meleager. She married Andræmon.]

(992) [Podalirius.—Ver. 735. The brother of Machaon. See the Tristia Book v. El. xiii. 1. 32.]

(993) [Calchas.—Ver. 737. See the Metamorphoses.]

(994) [Automeden.—Ver. 738. The son of Diores. He was the charioted of Achilles.]

(995) [Upon his spoil—Ver. 744. It was the custom to write inscriptions on the spoil. See the Notes to the Fasti, Book ii. 1. 663.]

FOOTNOTES OF BOOK- THE THIRD

(1001) [Penthesilea.'—Ver. 2. See the 21st Epistle, 1.118, and the Note.]

(1002) [Dione.—Ver. 3. See the Fasti, Book ii. 1. 461, and the Note.]

(1003) [Son of Atreus.—Ver. 11. 'Helen was unfaithful to Menelaus, while Clytemnestra killed Agamemnon.]

(1004) [Son of Oeclus.—Ver. 13. See the Metamorphoses, Book viii. 1. 317, ind the Note.]

(1005) [From Phylace.—Ver. 17. See the Epistle of Laodamia to Protesilaius.]

(1006) [Son of Pheres.—Ver. 19. See the Pontic Epistles, Book iii. El. i. L 106, and the Note.]

(1007) [And in place of—Ver. 20. See the 111th line of the same Elegy, and the Note. Also the Tristia, Book v. El. xiv. 1. 38.]

(1008) [My skiff.—Ver. 26. 'Cymba.' See the Amores, Book iii. El. vi. 1. 4, and the Note.]

(1009) [Another bride.—Ver. 34. Jason deserted Medea for Creusa.]

(1010) [Nine journies.—Ver. 37. See the Epistle of Phyllis to Demophoon.]

(1011) [Two treatises.—Ver. 47. His former books on the Art of Love.]

(1012) [Who before had uttered.—Ver. 49. He alludes to the Poet Stesichorus, on whose lips a nightingale was said to have perched and sung, when he was a child. Pliny relates that he wrote a poem, inveighing bitterly against Helen, in which he called her the firebrand of Troy, on which he was visited with blindness by her brothers, Castor and Pollux, and did not recover his sight till he had recanted in his Palinodia, which he composed in her praise. Suidas says, that Stesichorus composed thirty, six books of Poems. Helen was born at Therapnæ, a town of Laconia.]

(1013) [Your own privileges.—Ver. 58. 'Sua' seems to mean the privileges sanctioned and conceded by the law, probably to those females who were in the number of the 'professae.']

(1014) [No door.—Ver. 71. So Horace says, in his address to Lydia, Book i. Ode i. 25; 'Less frequently do the wanton youths shake your joined windows with many a blow, and no longer deprive thee of sleep, and the door adheres to its threshold.']

(1015) [Bestrewed with roses.—Ver. 72. See line 528: in the last Book Lucretius speaks of the admirers of damsels anointing their doors with M ointment made of sweet marjoram.]

(1016) [Hermione.—Ver. 86. According to Hesiod, Venus was the mother of three children by Mars, of whom Hermione was one.]

(1017) [May take up again.—Ver. 96. This is not the proper translation, of the passage; but the real meaning cannot be presented with a due regard to decorum.]

(1018) [I begin with dress.—Ver. 101. He plays upon the different meanings of the word 'cultus'; which means either 'dress,' or 'cultivation,' according as it is applied, to persons or land.]

(1019) [A great part.—Ver. 104. This is a more ungallant remark than we should have expected Ovid to make.]

(1020) [Of Phoebus.—Ver. 119. He alludes to the temple of Apollo, on the Palatine Hill, where Augustus and Tiberius resided.]

(1021) [And choice shells.—Ver. 124. He alludes to pearls which grow in the shell of the pearl oyster, and are found in the Persian Gulf and the Indian Ocean.]

(1022) [By the moles.—Ver. 126. He alludes to the stupendous moles which the Romans fabricated, as breakwaters, at their various bathing-places on the coast of Italy. See the Odes of Horace, Book iii. ode 1.]

(1023) [Round features.—Ver. 139. See the Pontic Epistles, Book iii Ep. iii. 1. 15, and the Note.]

(1024) [Figure of the tortoise.—Ver. 147. Salmasius thinks that the 'galerus,' or 'wig of false hair,' is alluded to in this passage. Others think that a coif or fillet of net-work is alluded to. He probably means a mode of dressing the hair in the shape of a lyre, with horns on each side projecting outwards. Mercury, the inventor of the lyre, was born on Mount Cyllene, in Arcadia.]

(1025) [The waves.—Ver. 148. Juvenal mentions a mode of dressing the hair to a great height by rows of false curls.]

(1026) [The herbs from Germany.—Ver. 163. He alludes, probably, to herbs brought from Germany, which were burnt for the purpose of making a soap used in turning the hair of a blonde colour. See the Amores, Book i. El. xiv. 1. 1, and the Note.]

(1027) [For money—Ver. 166. See 1. 45 of the above Elegy.]

(1028) [The eyes of Hercules.—Ver. 168. He means that the wig-makers'shops were in the neighbourhood of the Temple of Hercules Musagetes, in the Flaminian Circus. See the Sixth Book of the Fasti, 1. 801.]

(1029) [Gold flounces.—Ver. 169. 'Segmenta' are probably broad flounces to the dresses inlaid with plates of gold, or gold threads embroidered on them.]

(1030) [On one's person.—Ver. 127. Like our expression, 'To carry a fortune on one's back.']

(1031) [That art said.—Ver. 175. He refers to the colour of the Ram with the Golden Fleece, that bore Helle and Phryxus over the Hellespont.]

(1032) [Resembles the waves.—Ver. 177. He evidently alluded to dresses which resemble the surface of the waves, and which we term 'watered'; and which the Romans called 'undulatae,' from 'unda,' a 'wave.' Varro makes mention of 'undulatæ togæ.' Some Commentators, however, fancy that he alludes here to colour, meaning 'glaucus,' or 'sea-green,' which Lucretius also calls ' thalassinus.']

(1033) [Amaryllis.—Ver. 183. See the last Book, 1. 267, and the Note.]

(1034) [And wax.—Ver. 184. Plautus mentions the 'Carinarii,' who dyed garments of a waxen, or yellow colour]

(1035) [Seriphos.—Ver. 192. See the Metamorphoses, Book v. 1. 242, and the Note.]

(1036) [Shocking goat.—Ver. 193. See the Note to 1. 522: of the First Book.]

(1037) [Application of wax.—Ver. 199. Wax is certainly used as a cosmetic, but 'creta' seems to be a preferable reading, as chalk in a powdered state was much used for adding to the fairness of the complexion. Ovid would hardly recommend a cosmetic of so highly injurious a tendency as melted wax.]

(1038) [The eye-brows.—Ver. 201. We learn from Juvenal, that the colour of them was heightened by punctures with a needle being filled with soot.]

(1039) [And the little patch.—Ver. 202. 'Aluta' means 'skin made soft by means of alum.' It is difficult to discover what it means here, whether 'a patch' made of a substance like gold-beater's skin, somewhat similar to those used in the days of the Spectator; or a liquid cosmetic, such as Pliny calls 'calliblepharum,' 'an aid to the eye-brows.' He seems to use the word 'sinceras' in its primitive sense, 'without wax'; which recommendation certainly would contradict the common reading, 'cera,' in the 199th line.]

(1040) [To mark the eyes.—Ver. 203. To heighten the colour of the eyelashes, ashes (and probably charcoal) were u"ed by the Roman women. Saffron also was used. A black paint, made of pulverized antimony, is used by the women in the East, at the present day, to paint their eyebrows black. It is called 'surme,' and was also used at ancient Rome. Cydnus was a river of Cilicia.]

(1041) [A little treatise.—Ver. 205. He alludes to his book, 'On the care of the Complexion,' of which a fragment remains.]

(1042) [Of the cesypum.—Ver. 213. The filthy cosmetic called 'cesypum,' was prepared from the wool of those parts of the body where the sheep perspired most; it was much used for embellishing the complexion. Pliny mentions the sheep of Athens as producing the best. It had a strong rank smell. The red colour, which was used by the Roman ladies for giving a bloom to the skin, was prepared from a moss called 'fucus'; from which, in time, all kinds of paint received the name of 'fucus.']

(1043) [Of the deer.—Ver. 215. Pliny speaks highly of the virtues of stag's marrow. It probably occupied much the same position in estimation, that bear's grease does at the present day.]

(1044) [Myron.—Ver. 219. There were two sculptors of this name: one a native of Lycia, the other of Eleuthera.]

(1045) [Beautiful statue.—Ver. 223. He alludes to that of Venus Anadyomene, or rising from the sea, which was made by Praxiteles, and was often copied by the sculptors of Greece and Rome.]

(1046) [Pierces her arms.—Ver. 240. See a similar passage in the Amores. Book i. El. xiv. 1. 16.]

(1047) [Toilet in the temple.—Ver. 244. He tells those who have not fine heads of hair, to be as careful in admitting any men to see their toilet, as the devotees of Bona Dea were to keep away all males from her solemnities.]

(1048) [Sidonian fair.—Ver. 252. Europa was a Phoenician by birth.]

(1049) [With the clothes.—Ver. 226. See the Amores, Book i. El. iv. 1.48, and the Note.]

(1050) [With purple stripes.'—Ver. 269. Commentators are at a loss to know what 'tingere virgis' means; some suggest, 'to wear garments with red 'virgæ,' or 'stripes,'while others think that it means 'to tint the skin with fine lines of a purple colour.' It is thought by some that vermilion is here alluded to, while others suppose that the juice of the red flowers, or berries of the 'vaccinium,' is meant.]

(1051) [The Pharian fish.—Ver. 270. The intestines and dung of the crocodile, 'the Pharian' or 'Egyptian fish,' are here referred to. We learn from Pliny that these substances were used by the females at Rome as a cosmetic, to add to the fairness of the complexion, and to take away freckles from the skin.]

(1052) [Small pads are suitable.—Ver. 273 'Analectides,' or 'Analectrides,' (the correct reading is doubtful) were pads, or stuffings, of flock, used in cases of high shoulders or prominent shoulder-blades.]

(1053) [And let the girth.—Ver. 274. He alludes to the 'strophium,' which distantly resembled the stays of the present day, and was a girdle, or belt, worn by women round the breast and over the interior tunic or chemise. From an Epigram of Martial, it seems to have been usually made of leather. Becker thinks that there was a difference between the 'fascia' and the 'strophium.']

(1054) [At a distance.—Ver. 278. One of the very wisest of his suggestions.]

(1055) [Umbrian.—Ver. 303. The Umbrians were a people of the Marsi, in the north of Italy. They were noted for their courage, and the rusticity of their manners.]

(1056) [The son of Sisyphus.—Ver. 313. He here alludes to a scandalous story among the ancients, that Ulysses was the son of Anticlea, by Sisyphus the robber, who had carried her off, and not by Laertes, her husband.]

(1057) [The wax.—Ver. 314. By the advice of Circe, Ulysses filled the ears of his companions with melted wax, that they might not hear the songs of the Sirens.]

(1058) [The measures of the Nile.—Ver. 318. These airs were sung by Egyptian girls, with voluptuous attitudes, and were much esteemed by the dissolute Romans. These Egyptian singers were, no doubt, the forerunners of the 'Alme' of Egypt at the present day. The Nautch girls and Bayaderes of the East Indies are a kindred race.]

(1059) [Plectrum.—Ver. 319. See the Metamorphoses, Book ii. 1. 601, and the Note; also the Epistle of Briseïs, 1. 118, and the Note.]

(1060) [Thy mother.—Ver. 323. Amphion and Zethuswere the sons of Jupiter and Antiope. Being carried off by her uncle Lycus, Antiope was entrusted to his wife Dirce. When her sons grew up, they fastened Dirce to wild oxen, by which she was tom to pieces. Amphion was said to have built the walls of Thebes by the sound of his lyre.]

(1061) [Arion.—Ver. 326. See the Fasti, Book ii. 1. 79.]

(1062) [The festive psaltery.—Ver. 327. Suidas tells us that 'naulium,' or 'nablium,' was a name of the psaltery. Josephus says that it had twelve strings. Strabo remarks that the name was of foreign origin.]

(1063) [Callimachus.—Ver. 329. See the Amores, Book ii. El. iv. 1. 19: and the Pontic Epistles, Book iv. Ep. xvi. 1. 32, and the Notes of the passages.]

(1064) [Poet of Cos.—Ver. 330. The poet Philetas. He flourished in the time of Philip and Alexander the Great. Anacreon was a lyric poet of Teios, and a great admirer of the juice of the grape.]

(1065) [Or him, through whom.—Ver. 332. Some think that he means Menander, from whom Terence borrowed many of his scenes; he probably alludes to the Phormio of Terence, where the old men, Chremes and Demipho, are deceived by Geta, the cunning slave. See the Tristia, Book ii. 1. 359: and 69.]

(1066) [Propertius.'—Ver. 333. See the Tristia, Book ii. 1. 465, and the Note.]

(1067) [Tibullus.—Ver. 334. See the Amores, Book iii. EL ix.]

(1068) [Varro.—Ver. 335. See the Pontic Epistles, Book iv. Ep. xvi. 1. 21; and the Amores, Book i. El. xv. 1. 21, and the Notes to the passages.]

(1069) [Lofty Rome.—Ver. 338. He refers here to the Æneid of Virgil.]

(1070) [Two sides.—Ver. 342. Both the males and the females.]

(1071) [Composition.—Ver. 346. He takes to himself the credit of being the inventor of Epistolary composition.]

(1072) [Masters of posture.—Ver. 351. These persons, who were also called 'ludii,' or 'histrlones,' required great suppleness of the sides, for the purpose of aptly assuming expressive attitudes; for which reason he calls them 'artifices lateris.' See the First Book, 1. 112; and the Tristia, Book ii, 1. 497, and the Note.]

(1073) [Which she must call for.—Ver. 356. Probably at the game of 'duodecim seripta,' or 'twelve points,' like our backgammon; sets of three 'tesseræ,' or dice, were used for throwing; he recommends her to learn the game, and to know on what points to enter when taken up, and what throws to call for. See the last Book, 1. 203; and the Tristia, Book ii. 1. 473, and the Note.]

(1074) [The pieces.—Ver. 357. See the Note to 1. 207, in the last Book.]

(1075) [The warrior, too.—Ver. 359. He alludes to one of the principal pieces, whose fate depends upon another.]

(1076) [Let the smooth balls.—Ver. 361. He seems to allude here to a game played by putting marbles (which seems to be the meaning of 'pilæ leves,' 'smooth balls,') into a net with the month open, and then taking them out one by one without moving any of the others.]

(1077) [Kind of game.—Ver. 363. These two lines do not seem to be connected with the game mentioned in 1. 365, but rather to refer to that mentioned in 1. 355.]

(1078) [A little table receives.}—Ver. 365. This game is mentioned in the Tristia, Book ii. 1. 481. It seems to resemble the simple game played by schoolboys on the slate, and known among them as tit-tat-to.]

(1079) [No trusting.—Ver. 377. On account of the continued run of bad luck.]

(1080) [Flying ball.'—Ver. 380. See the Tristia, Book ii. 1. 485-6, and the Note.]

(1081) [The Virgin.—Ver. 385. This was near the Campus Martius. See the Fasti, Book i. 1. 464; and the Pontic Epistles, Book i. Ep. viii. 1. 38, and the Note.]

(1082) [Etrurian.—Ver. 386. The Tiber flowed through ancient Etruria.]

(1083) [The Virgin.—Ver. 388. He alludes to the heat while the sun is passing through the Constellation Virgo.]

(1084) [Parætonium.—Ver. 390. See the Amores, Book ii. El. xiii. 1. 7, and the Note. He alludes to the victory of Augustus over Antony and Cleopatra, at Actium; on which the conqueror built the temple of Apollo on the Palatine hill.]

(1085) [The suter and the wife.—Ver. 391. Livia, the wife, and Octavia, the sister of Augustus, are referred to.]

(1086) [His son-in-law.—Ver. 392. The allusion is to M. Agrippa, the husband of Julia, the daughter of Augustus; after the defeat of the younger Pompey, Augustus presented him with a naval crown. A Portico built by Augustus was called by his name.]

(1087) [Memphian heifer.—Ver. 393. See the Amores, Book i. El. viii. 1. 74.]

(1088) [Frequent the three Theatres.—Ver. 394. He probably alludes to the theatres of Pompey, Balbus, and Marcellus, as they are mentioned by Suetonius as the 'trina theatra.']

(1089) [Glowing wheels.—Ver. 396. See the Amores, Book iii. El. ii.]

(1090) [Thamyras.—Ver. 399. He was a Thracian poet, who challenged the Muses to sing, and, according to Homer, was punished with madness. Diodorus Siculus says that he lost his voice, while the Roman poets state that he lost his sight. Amoebeus was a famous lute-player of Athens.]

(1091) [Of Cos.—Ver. 401. See the Pontic Epistles, Book iv. Ep. i. 1. 29.]

(1092) [Poets were.—Ver. 405. Euripides was the guest of Archelaüs king of Macedonia, Anacreon of Polycrates king of Samos, and Pindar and Bacchilides of Hiero king of Sicily.]

(1093) [Placed near to thee.—Ver. 410. According to some accounts, the ashes of Ennius were deposited in the tomb of the Scipios, by the older of his friend Scipio Africanus.]

(1094) [Its own Priam.—Ver. 440. Priam and Antenor advised that Helen should be restored to Menelaus.]

(1095) [Liquid nard.—Ver. 443. There were two kinds of nard, the 'foliated,' and the 'spike' nard. It was much esteemed as a perfume by the Romans.]

(1096) [Narrow belt.—Ver. 444. He probably means a girdle that fitted tightly, and caused the 'toga' to set in many creases. See the Notes to the Fasti, Book v. 1. 675.]

(1097) [And many a ring.—Ver. 446. 'alter et alter.' Literally, one and another.]

(1098) [Some thief.—Ver. 447. Among its other refinements, Rome seems to have had its swell mob.]

(1099) [Thou, Venus—Ver. 451. This temple is referred to in the First Book, 1. 81—87. Its vicinity was much frequented by courtesans.]

(1101) [You, ye Goddesses.—Ver. 452. He probably alludes to the Nymphs whose statues were near the Appian aqueduct, mentioned in the 81st Une of the First Book. The Delphin Editor absolutely thinks that the 'pro-fessæ,' or courtesans, are themselves alluded to as the 'Appiades Deæ.']

(1102) [Theseus.—Ver. 457. Who deserted Ariadne.]

(1103) [Of Inachus.—Ver. 464. Isis, or To. Seo the Metamorphoses, Bk. i.]

(1104) [To deceive your husbands.—Ver. 484. It is not improbable that 'viros' here means merely 'keepers,' and not 'husbands,' especially as he alludes to their being without the privilege of the 'vitta,' which the matrons wore.]

(1105) [Two hands.—Ver. 496. He means, that the writing of the lover must be quite erased before she pens her answer on the same tablets.]

(1106) [Hence, avaunt.—Ver. 505. See the Fasti, Book vi. 1. 696. * Laying aside his foils.—Ver. 515. The 'rudis' was a stick, which soldiers and persons exercising used in mimic combat, probably like our foil or singlestick.]

(1107) [With Tecmessa.—Ver. 517. She was taken captive by Ajax, and probably had good reason to be sorrowful.]

(1108) [The twig of vine.—Ver. 527. He alludes to the Centurions, who had the power of inflicting corporal punishment, from which circumstance their badge of office was a vine sapling.]

(1109) [Nemesis.—Ver. 536. Nemesis was the mistress of Tibullus. See the Amores, Book iii. El. ix. Cynthia was the mistress of Propertius and Lycoris of Gallus.]

(1110) [Shut your door.—Ver. 587. He addresses the husband, whom he supposes to be wearied with satiety.]

(1111) [Than even Thais.—Ver. 604. Thais seems to have been a common name with the courtesans of ancient times. Terence, in his Eunuchus, introduces one of that name, who is pretty much of the free and unrestrained character here depicted.]

(1112) [Lictor's rod.—Ver. 615. This conferred freedom on the slave who was touched with it. See the Fasti, Book vi. 1. 676, and the Note, lie means, that free-born women are worthy to become wives; but 'libertinæ,' or 'freed-women,' are only fit to become 'professæ,' or 'courtesans,' when they may sin with impunity, so far as the laws are concerned.]

(1113) [Broad girth.—Ver. 622. This seems to be the kind of belt mentioned in line 274.]

(1114) [Stalk of wetted flax.—Ver. 629. According to the common reading, this will mean that the letter is to be written on blank paper, with a stalk of wetted flax; which writing will afterwards appear, when a black substance is thrown upon it. Heinsius insists that the passage is corrupt, and suggests that 'alumine nitri' is the correct reading; in which case it would mean that alum water is to be used instead of ink. Vessius tells us that alum water, mixed with the juice of the plant 'tithymalum,' was used for the purposes of secret correspondence.]

(1115) [Good Goddess.—Ver. 637. The debauched Clodius was detected as being present at these rites, in a female dress.]

(1116) [The false key, too, tells. — Ver. 643. He plays upon the double meaning of the words, 'adultéra clavis,' which properly signifies 'a false key.']

(1117) [Even though. — Ver. 646. 'Even though you should have to go to the expense of providing the rich wines of Spain for the purpose.']

(1118) [Even she. — Ver. 663. He alludes to the accommodating lady mentioned in line 641.]

(1119) [Has she filled. — Ver. 666. See his address to Cypassis, in the Amores, Book ii. El. viii.]

(1120) [Lemnian dames. — Ver. 672. See the introduction to the Epistle from Hypsipyle to Jason.]

(1121) [Cephaltis. — Ver. 695. This story is also related in the Seventh Book of the Metamorphoses.]

(1122) [The quinces. — Ver. 705. These are called 'cydonia,' from Cydon, city of Crete.]

(1123) [Cyllenian God. — Ver. 725. Cephalus was said to be the son of Mercury; but, according to one account, which is followed by Ovid in the Metamorphoses, Deioneus was his father.]

(1124) [Her breath. — Ver. 746. See the corresponding passage in the Metamorphoses, Book vii. 1. 861. It was the custom for the nearest relative to catch the breath of the dying person in the mouth.]

(1125) [With your fingers. — Ver. 755.. Perhaps he means in moderato quantities at a time, and not in whole handfuls. See the Note to the First Book, 1. 577.]

(1126) [And do not first. — Ver. 757. He seems to irs two precepts here; first, they are not to eat so much at home as to take away all appetite at the banquet, as that would savour of affectation, and be an act of rudeness to the host. On the other hand, he warns them not to stuff as long as they are able, but rather to leave off with an appetite. The passage, however, is hopelessly corrupt, and is capable of other interpretations.]

(1127) [Perform their duty. — Ver. 764. 'Constent,' literally. 'Will stand together.']

(1128) [The swans. — Ver. 899. He also alludes to them in the Metamorphoses, as drawing the car of Venus, though that office was more generally assigned by the Poets to doves.]

9 789358 592092